DESERT OF HARDSHIP
WATER OF HOPE

DESERT OF HARDSHIP
WATER OF HOPE

**RELYING ON GOD
IN DIFFICULT RELATIONSHIPS**

Jill Briscoe & Judy Briscoe Golz

For Her. For God. For Real.
faithfulwoman.com

Faithful Woman is an imprint of
Cook Communications Ministries, Colorado Springs, Colorado 80918
Cook Communications, Paris, Ontario
Kingsway Communications, Eastbourne, England

© 2002 by Jill Briscoe and Judy Golz. All rights reserved.

Printed in the United States of America.

1 2 3 4 5 6 7 8 9 10 Printing/Year 05 04 03 02

Unless otherwise noted, all Scripture references are from The Holy Bible, New International Version (NIV), copyright © 1973, 1978, 1984, International Bible Society. Used by permission of Zondervan Bible Publishers.

Senior Editor: Janet Lee
Cover design: Image Studios
Interior design: Image Studios

CIP data application filed

No part of this book may be reproduced without written permission, except for brief quotations in books and critical reviews. For information, write Cook Communications Ministries, 4050 Lee Vance View, Colorado Springs, Colorado, 80918.

CONTENTS

Preface 9

Introduction 11

Chapter 1 — Confusion 13

Chapter 2 — Conflicts 25

Chapter 3 — Coping 37

Chapter 4 — Community 55

Chapter 5 — Change 65

Chapter 6 — Communion 79

Chapter 7 — Caring..95

Chapter 8 — Commitment 107

We dedicate these pages
to the Hagars and Ishmaels of this world.
We hope they will find within these pages
grace to go on against the odds.

PREFACE

Judy and I have a huge concern for parents, like Hagar, who find themselves with all the props knocked out from under them; and the children, like Ishmael, who are victims of their circumstances. We want to encourage from God's Word people who are raw from life's bruisings.

This study reproduces a seminar we teach. Judy's contributions are indicated in italics. And we have together compiled the application exercises at the end of each chapter. Talk Time can be used to generate discussions in small groups, Bible studies, and Sunday school classes or in one-on-one discipleship. Think Time gives additional Scripture for personal or group reflection. Prayer Time gives practical guides for personal or corporate prayer. Action Time gives churches and groups practical ideas on how to reach out to those in need.

We hope you can catch the flavor of the story, apply some of the principles to your life, and find grace to go on, if necessary, "against the odds" in the power of the Lord.

Jill Briscoe

DESERT OF HARDSHIP, WATER OF HOPE

INTRODUCTION

When one of your relationships falls apart, how do you survive the crash? As the family crumbles and broken people are faced with broken promises that take two to mend, more and more complex relationships are thrust on us. It takes an awful lot of energy to survive. This is what this book is all about.

Joseph died before Jesus ever left home to begin His ministry.

So Jesus knew what it was to be part of a single-parent family.

He was exposed to sibling rivalry, hostility from brothers, and watched His mother despised and rejected by His society.

He Himself was called a bastard.

Yes, Jesus understands the Hagars and Ishmaels of this world.

Jesus understands children like Ishmael lying under their broom trees, wishing they could die because it hurts so much!

Children who are not without scars!

Deep wounds marked Hagar's soul as well;

they were noted by heaven, cared for and prayed about by Jesus.

Hagar and Christ's own dear mother would have been good friends.

Both understood how cruel and unkind humanity can be.

Both lost husbands and both were left alone with children to raise.

Both cried out to the Lord and found Him to be a very present help in trouble.

Hagar, rejected and destitute, cast herself on God and found His grace to be sufficient.

God is fully empathetic with mothers like Hagar who think there's nothing left to live for.

God raised Jesus from the dead and made Him a King of a mighty kingdom where He lives with the power to look after all the Hagars and Ishmaels of this wild world.

So when you get down—so far down you think you want to die—look up at the King's face, His hands, His feet, His side, and remember your Lord Jesus is not without scars!

CHAPTER ONE
CONFUSION

God wants you to know that you can make it "against the odds." You may feel the whole world and the forces of hell itself are against you, but He wants you to understand that the forces of heaven are for you! "If God is for us, who can be against us?" (Romans 8:31) the Apostle Paul asks, and he should know what he was talking about. He made it against the odds, I would say! Listen to the catalogue of his troubles:

> I have worked much harder, been in prison more frequently, been flogged more severely, and been exposed to death again and again. Five times I received from the Jews forty lashes minus one. Three times I was beaten with rods, once I was stoned, three times I was shipwrecked, I spent a night and a day in the open sea, I have been constantly on the move. I have been in danger from rivers, in danger from bandits, in danger from my own countrymen, in danger from Gentiles; in danger in the city, in danger in the country, in danger at sea; and in danger from false brothers. I have labored and toiled and have often gone without sleep; I have known hunger and thirst and have often gone without food; I have been cold and naked. Besides everything else, I face daily the pressure of my concern for all the churches. (2 Corinthians 11:23-28)

Yet Paul could sincerely say, "But thanks be to God! He gives us the victory through our Lord Jesus Christ" (1 Corinthians 15:57). This is not to suggest that God will kiss every hurt better but rather that He'll help and enable us to cope with the hurt.

What sort of things am I talking about? Not Paul's troubles but those family wounds and relational traumas that can cause the deepest emotional pain of all. Let me tell you a story.

The Story
The little girl was confused. Grandma was coming to stay. The problem was that the little girl seemed to have an awful lot of grandmas. Her mommy had told her it had something to do with a divorce. She hadn't minded one little bit at first. Who wouldn't want more than one grandma? Grandmas were beautiful human beings. They smiled a lot, had comfortable laps to sit on while they read you a story, and had time to listen to little people because they didn't have to be doing all the other things that big people did!

But the little girl soon discovered acquiring more and more grandparents wasn't all that great. She tried to learn their many names by heart, but it was very confusing and sometimes she got them all mixed up! Her mommy tried to help her by reminding her that it wasn't Helen but "Gran" that was coming to visit on a particular day. The little girl wanted to make quite sure she got it right this time, so she began to practice the grandparent's name quietly all by herself as she rocked to and fro on her little wooden horse. "It's Gran, not Helen," she whispered to her rocking horse. "Remember that it's Gran, not Helen!" It was small wonder that that particular grandma found herself addressed on that particular visit by that particular four-year-old as "Not Helen!"

We might not be small children, but many of us can sadly relate to this little girl. It's hard enough to respond to a few people who belong to us, without being presented with total strangers who expect us to relate with perfect ease and great aplomb at any given time of the day or night!

And what about the grandparents caught up in the same drama? Where do they fit into the story? Some fit in very well indeed, bringing their maturity and wisdom to bear on their children's struggles. Many bear the weight of their private grief well, while others feel the odds are too great. They crumble, feeling useless and helpless, their advice spurned, and their love rejected. Worst of all, some discover divorce touches their lives in the most poignant way as they lose touch with their beloved grandchildren! As the "couples" move away to different parts of the country and begin their lives over again, distance erects barriers that an older person's small bank allowance can't possibly meet. Some, however, grapple with a different problem. They experience an unexpected togetherness as their single-parent children and their grandchildren, discovering a new poverty, move in. Grandmas and grandpas often move over, making room in their retirement to begin parenting all over again.

The Broken Family
All over the world's playroom, relationships lie battered like broken toys. Some people try to explain what happened when the toys were dropped; others lecture the children on being careless, pointing out they have had a part in the destruction. Still others try to mend the unmendable, refusing to face the fact that some toys are broken beyond repair. And always there are tears! If only real people were toys and the world itself was indeed a playroom, then the tears would soon be dried and a "better doll" purchased to replace the last. But these broken relationships that are mangled and smashed on the floor of our dreams are not plastic playthings purchased with loose change but living, breathing parts of our lives.

In other words, people's wounds need binding up with the bandages of blessings that appear to be quite out of stock in the emergency room of life! How do people manage to cope with the low blows of life without a spiritual resource? The problem is that so many people turn to God only when things are falling apart.

The God of Order
There is so much confusion in the world that we need to ask the God of peace to bring order into the chaos. He can and will help us in an emergency, but that's not the way to live a sensible and healthy life. We need to be daily drawing on His infinite wisdom and strength in order to stay well and avoid the spiritual ambulance coming to our door! God brings order and calm to our hearts, which in turn is transferable to those who live with and around us.

Remember the story of Jesus and His disciples caught in a storm on the Sea of Galilee? There were other little boats with them. The Lord was asleep in the back of the boat; however, the disciples woke Him up, asking if He cared that they were all about to drown (Mark 4:36-38). Jesus calmed the storm and rebuked the disciples for their lack of faith. The men were dumbfounded. "Who is this?" they asked. "Even the wind and the waves obey Him!"

The storm brought trouble to all of them, just as the calming of the sea brought peace to all of them. When we put our trust in the God of the storm, even the little ships around us will feel the calming effect. A person's personal faith helps to make faith personal for others.

These days families are struggling to remember what faith in the God of the storm is all about and what families are supposed to be. It wasn't too long ago that a couple getting married reiterated their vows with sincerity and belief that even though worse things happened to them rather than *better* things, *poorer* times came calling, *sickness* rather than *health* was waiting for them around the corner of their tomorrows, they would see it all through together till death them did part! Today few stand at the altar or in front of a justice of the peace with much more than a starry-eyed fragile "hope" that the marriage will last at all. More than a few have decided not to have children at all in case their liaison doesn't work out. But others go ahead even though many bring with them lots of baggage from their own broken backgrounds. What can they do, and where can they go to find help?

In a place called heaven in a time called eternity, a being called God looks down on a hurting world with great compassion. He fully realizes this terrible situation demands His immediate attention!

But people are too busy to prepare room for Him. We do not readily see what God has to do with our earthly problem. It's as if we can't see the forest for the trees, or to change the metaphor, we can't see God for the giants. People's relational problems are gigantic—as big as Goliath.

Goliath, who was nine feet tall was a Philistine. At this time in history, the Philistines were fighting the Israelites. However, no one in the Israelite armies had been able to
kill this giant. One day David, the youngest son of Jesse, was sent to the battlefield to find out how the battle was progressing. When David arrived and saw Goliath, he told King Saul that he would kill the giant. Saul dressed David in his own armor. However, David did not wear the armor or take the king's sword because he wasn't used to these things.

Instead, he took five smooth stones and his sling. When David went out to face Goliath, the giant was angry to see someone so young who wasn't dressed for battle. Yet, the first stone that David propelled from his sling killed the giant.

How do you fight your Goliaths? Do you have one large giant that is in your way, or are there many giants to overcome? Do you dress yourself in other people's solutions or do you, like David, use the resources that God has given you?

This is a story of how two ordinary people, Hagar and Ishmael, overcame the giants in their lives. Fighting against the odds Hagar and Ishmael had their own grim battles. However, like David discovering his five smooth stones, they discovered that God had provided resources right at hand.

Redemptive Relationship

As we will see, the first resource that was available to Hagar and Ishmael was a relationship with God. What sort of God can we trust to help us? The God of relationships! He made us like Him. He who is a Trinity enjoys a perfect, unbroken relationship within the Godhead, and when He created humankind, He made them after His image. That is, He made us like Himself with the capacity for a relationship and friendship with Himself and with each other.

Do you have a personal relationship with God? You need to make friends with Him too. He has taken the initiative; He died on the cross to make things right. This friendship with Himself that He offers is not to be taken lightly. It comes at a cost so great it can hardly be talked about! It took His death to enable Him to offer you life.

Who knows the time, the place, the sacred moment when Abram heard the sound of the Lord God walking in his garden? Yet one day there was a heartfelt response from
Abram and he became the friend of God! He came to faith—began to trust—totally, gladly, obediently. Early in the morning, at midday, and until midnight he was God's man. The friendship grew, developed, and matured. It was done; it was settled! A man with a sinful heart had reached out to grasp the hand of God and eagerly accepted His strength and grace. He believed the Lord's precious promises were for him and his family. Abraham "believed God," we are told in the New Testament, "and it was credited to him as righteousness" (James 2:23). Everything

that had been wrong in Abraham's life was covered by God's free forgiveness. Faith was put to work as the man leaned hard on God's arm of friendship. Things didn't always go perfectly for him, but just imagine what Abraham's life would have been like without his fantastic relationship with God! Abraham teaches us many things, not least the fact that when you are right with God, *all* your human relationships feel the impact.

God has helped me so much with my relationships. Before I became a Christian, I had few friends. I believed God was a supreme being, but hardly "supreme" enough to warrant a second of my attention and barely "being" enough in my mind to be who He wanted to be in my life. Consequently, I was on my own. Without His friendly companionship, I was at a loss to know how to be a friendly companion to others. My friends were "fair-weather," like myself. Like finds like, you know, and I chose empty-headed "fun mates" whose shallow lives (like mine) allowed nothing deeper to develop between us than surface banalities and trivial pursuits. Of course, I was unaware that this was the case. Never having experienced anything better, I felt no obligation to try harder where friendship was concerned. Then I became a believer and found I had a friend! He was a friend who began to show me depths of human experience in the spiritual realm that opened up a whole new expectation about my other friendships.

Friendship, I discovered, was a large room, empty when you first entered it but able to be furnished with my daily doings for others. When made ready, friendship was a room where folk would feel welcomed, kick their shoes off, and know they had come home. Women at my college began to come around me, reaching out for attention. Loners who didn't really want to be loners asked me how come I had suddenly become so popular, and selfish women who had known me before saw the difference and wanted to know "why." I was able to tell them so little, but the little I told them was a whole lot more than I had ever had to tell anyone before! *Jesus loved me; we were friends,* I explained! We spent time together and talked—oh, how we talked! He listened a lot, and because God listened to me, I began to understand that that's one thing real friends can do for each other. When you learn to listen, it won't be long before lonely people come around you like bees around a honey pot.

What a difference that discovery made in my relationships! I soon realized I had lost most of my fair-weather friends. Once I was converted, they acted as though a tornado had hit me, instead of realizing the sun was shining on my head! God, however, helped me salvage one or two of these friendships and added others that became the real solid companions of my life. These are people I still keep in touch with forty years later because we learned together how to listen and love each other. God is indeed the God of lasting relationships, and to know Him is to begin to know how to build eternal bonds of commitment with people.

A personal relationship with God brings God into all our personal relationships. As He lives out His life in our lives, our hands, feet, eyes, ears, and heart become His. If He is first in our lives, we will turn to Him—not as a last resort, but as a first thought before trouble comes.

DESERT OF HARDSHIP, WATER OF HOPE

 **TALK TIME**

1. Choose from the following phrases one that strikes you and say whether or not you agree with it.

People's wounds need binding up with the bandages of blessings that appear to be quite out of stock in the emergency room of life!
A person's personal faith helps to make faith personal for others.
When you learn how to listen, it won't be long before lonely people come around.

2. Make up an acrostic of the reasons your life gets confusing. Your list may look like this:

   C — chronic ill health
   O — office
   N — no communication
   F — family fights
   U — undermined values
   S — soap operas
   I — indecision
   O — obstinacy
   N — no church

3. Next make a list of positives that could counteract the confusion in your life. Example:

   C — clear thinking
   O — ongoing good friendships
   N — not backing off
   F — firmness on moral issues
   U — understanding the people in the problem
   S — support systems
   I — inspiration
   O — order
   N — nurturing spiritual life

CONFUSION

 **THINK TIME**

On your own, look up the following verses that have to do with families. Think about them.

Genesis 2:23-25
Ephesians 5:22
Ephesians 5:25
Ephesians 6:1
Ephesians 6:4
2 Timothy 1:5

Choose one of the above verses. Write a paragraph to God about your reaction to it.

 **PRAYER TIME**

1. Pray generally for:
   Adults struggling in their marriages.
   Children struggling with the adults.
   Grandparents with their own struggles—that God will bring reconciliation, healing, help, council, strength to go on.

2. Pray through the Lord's Prayer together out loud.

3. Spend time praying for the following:

   Pray for all children and adults who, because of their backgrounds, have a wrong concept of "Father."
   Pray His kingdom will come into the hearts of unbelieving family members.
   Pray partners in marriage will be willing to do His will, not theirs.
   Pray for families in financial trouble and those who go hungry.
   Pray for forgiveness and reconciliation where there is bitterness.
   Pray people will avail themselves of the power of God that comes through having a personal relationship with Him.

 **ACTION TIME**

Purpose:
A church may be able to help prevent marital breakdown or intervene at early stages of marital problems.

Action ideas:
Premarital classes
Marriage enrichment classes
Consistent meetings with a pastor or lay couple after the wedding.

A plan for premarital classes:

A. Objectives
   Help couples to deal with issues that may lead to problems in their marriages.
   Help engaged individuals to become more aware of the type of person they are marrying.

B. Topics to cover
   Christian marriage
   Communication
   Resolving conflicts
   Finances
   Sexuality
   Parenting
   In-laws
   Others _____

C. Formats for covering the topics
   One-day workshop
   Sunday School classes
   Individual or group counseling sessions

D. Procedure
   Speak with the church leadership and determine which action idea might be the most appropriate for your church. (Assume the church

decides on the premarital classes.)
Decide who will implement the program (e.g., committee).
Decide which format for covering the topics will be most appropriate in your church.
Determine who will cover the topics.
a) One or two pastors could cover all topics.
b) Laypersons who have expertise in each area could present that specific material.
   (1) Christian marriage—pastor
   (2) Communication—pastor or professional in this area
   (3) Resolving Conflict—professional in this area
   (4) Finances—banker, accountant, or financial planner
   (5) Sexuality—gynecologist or obstetrician
   (6) Parenting—parents
   (7) In-laws—pastor or in-laws

Go to your Christian bookstore and find one or two texts for the class.

Assign readings and/or some written homework that couples could complete together each week.

Afterward, give the couples an opportunity to critique the content, format, and other areas of the course.
a) Give a short questionnaire.
b) Ask the couples to write down their general impressions.

DESERT OF HARDSHIP, WATER OF HOPE

CHAPTER TWO
CONFLICTS

Problems

Let's summarize a small part of the story of Hagar and Ishmael so that we can describe how having a relationship with God can make a difference when you are facing difficult problems. Beginning in Genesis 12, we see that God had a plan for Abram's life. God told the seventy-five-year old man to leave the comforts of his home and go out into the desert. He told Abram to wander in the wilderness until He told him that it was all right to settle down. Abram took his wife Sarai, his nephew Lot, and his family and obeyed the Lord. They traveled to Shechem, on to the east of Bethel, and toward the Negev. Because there was a famine, they headed down to Egyp.t

As they neared Egypt, Abram told his wife that he was frightened the Egyptians would see what a beautiful woman she was and kill him. Therefore, he asked Sarai to pretend she was his sister so the Egyptians would let him live. Well, Sarai went along with Abram's wild idea. Indeed, the Egyptians thought that Sarai was extremely beautiful. In fact, they told the Pharaoh about her. The Pharaoh agreed and promptly took Sarai into his palace so she could prepare to become his wife. In the meantime, the Pharaoh was very nice to Abram. He gave him cattle and servants. It might have been on this trip that Hagar, the maidservant was given or sold to Abram. Anyway, people in the palace became sick because "the Lord inflicted serious diseases on Pharaoh and his household because of Abram's wife Sarai" (Genesis 12:17). In time, Pharaoh discovered that Abram and Sarai were married. Incensed, he told the couple to pack up their belongings and leave. Abram, Sarai and Lot left Egypt and headed to the desert.

They traveled together into the wilderness and God prospered them. But there came a time when the grasslands couldn't handle both Abram's and Lot's cattle, and the herdsmen of both men began to quarrel (Genesis 13:7). Abram told his nephew that he didn't want a family rift. He suggested that Lot choose the piece of territory he wanted to live in and Abram would take the alternative. Lot agreed and chose the fertile plains. Abram moved to the hills. It was an unselfish thing for the patriarch to do because the plains certainly appeared to be more fertile and productive. However, it was apparently very important to Abram that he and Lot part in peace with their friendship intact.

A few years later, after Abram and Sarai had been through quite a few hardships, God appeared to Abram in a vision. Abram, still childless, was concerned that the chief servant in his household would become his heir. However, God told him that this wouldn't happen.

"Then the word of the Lord came to him: 'This man will not be your heir, but a son coming from your own body will be your heir.' He took him outside and said 'Look up at the heavens and count the stars—if indeed you can count them.' Then he said to him, 'So shall your offspring be'"(Genesis 15:4-5).

According to Abram and Sarai the one small problem with God's promise was that Sarai hadn't been able to conceive. Therefore, instead of waiting on the Lord, they decided to take matters into their own hands. Sarai came to Abram and told him that he should sleep with her maidservant, Hagar. If Hagar became pregnant, then the child would be raised as their son or daughter. Abram consented and slept with Hagar, and she conceived.

Like Sarai, one in six couples today is reported to be infertile; that's an extremely high percentage. Whatever the causes, the toll in human trauma is high. When a young couple is yearning for a baby and watching their dreams lie broken around them, tension is created between the couple, in the extended family, and among friends. "I found I couldn't stand seeing my friends get pregnant," confessed one such young woman to me. "It was out of the question to attend a baby shower. I felt awful feeling like that but couldn't seem to do anything about it!" Hopeful grandparents feel the same way.

It's hard to wait for God to intervene. How much easier to try to manipulate circumstances or the people under your control to bring your cherished dream to pass. Once a human being "uses" another human being for his or her own ends conflict is inevitable.

So Hagar's body was used as a solution to the problem of Sarai's infertility. In Genesis 16:2, Sarai says that her family will be built up from Hagar. Sarai uses Hagar as a baby machine, a human incubator.

When Abram and Sarai needed a warm body to achieve their ends, Hagar was there. She was young, she was strong, and she didn't have much option.

Many people think Bible stories like this one could never happen in our lifetime. Well, today we have the same thing happening; we call it surrogate parenting. In fact, a widely publicized case of surrogate parenting happened in the eighties and involved a New Jersey housewife, a biochemist, and his wife. They agreed that the housewife's medical expenses would be paid and she would be given $10,000. However, problems began when the mother decided she didn't want to give up her child. Perhaps the mother hadn't bargained on being unable to control her emotions. During the court battle of this case, an article in Time *magazine compared this situation with the story of Abram and Sarai. "Even the Bible offers a parallel. When his wife proved unable to conceive, Abram impregnated her handmaiden, Hagar, who bore Ishmael. There were hard feelings in the aftermath of that arrangement too" (Time, January 19, 1987).*

The Bible tells us that when Hagar knew that she was pregnant, she began to despise and belittle Sarai. Hagar found ways of letting Sarai know how she felt. Hagar went about her daily duties, but every time Sarai caught her eye, her color heightened. There was no escaping the gleam of triumph, the mocking smile, the daily reminder that she carried Abram's son. For once in her life she had possession of something Sarai wanted desperately.

In all honesty, each of us is guilty of acting like Hagar. Which of us has not belittled another by a rude action or saucy look? When our husbands come home late for dinner, we might let them know how we feel by slamming the oven door before plunking down the food in front of them. If our children are acting up, we give them a sizzling look, a silent message designed to stop them in their tracks.

One way we can really get revenge is to refuse to communicate about something the other party desperately wants to hear about. Who knows what it was that Hagar did to upset Sarai? It was at any rate eminently successful! Perhaps having told Sarai she was pregnant, she arrogantly kept her silence about the way her pregnancy was going. Silence can be one of the cruelest of retaliatory weapons. Whatever Hagar did, Sarai no doubt began to be sorry she hadn't waited for God to work it out His way!

How many times have we taken matters into our own hands? We may believe that God is big enough for some of our problems; however, there may be other situations that

we can't wait for Him to handle for us. There are other examples in the Bible of people taking matters into their own hands instead of waiting on the Lord and trusting in Him to deliver them from their situations. Remember the story about Moses leading the Children of Israel into the desert? It should have taken at the most only a year or two to travel from Egypt via the Sinai into Canaan. When Moses and the Children of Israel finally reached Kadesh Barnea, Moses was told by God to send men into Canaan to have a look around. It took these men forty days to explore the land. When they returned, they told everyone that the land was rich yet the people of the land were very powerful. So Moses decided that the people of Israel would attack. After all, God was on their side. Unfortunately, not everyone agreed with Moses. Those who had explored the land made sure that the people of Israel knew that they wouldn't stand a chance against the Canaanites. So the people of Israel rebelled. They actually thought that slavery in Egypt was a better option than going into Canaan. The Lord knew all about the rebelling of the Children of Israel. He decided that none of the people who were twenty years old or older and who had been counted in the census (except for Caleb and Joshua) would see the land that flowed with milk and honey. Instead they would wander in the desert for forty years.

After reviewing a story like this, we may think to ourselves that these people were blind for not trusting God. How could they think that by taking matters into their own hands they could make their lives better? He had been there for them so many times. Though we may not have such dramatic examples of how God has been there for us in our times of need, we all could give illustrations of the fact that things always work out best if we trust the Lord instead of putting our faith in our own abilities.

About one year after Greg and I were married, we had to make some very important decisions that would affect the next few years of our lives. Greg was finishing his graduate studies and beginning to look for a job. I wanted to go back to graduate school. Since both Chicago and New York held a lot of opportunities for both of us, we concentrated our efforts on looking into jobs and schools in these two locations. Then there was a period of waiting. Unfortunately, we didn't realize that this waiting period would overlap with five weeks of ministry in Australia with Mom. When I left, I hadn't heard from all the schools.

It was amazing that I could leave for the trip with such a feeling of peace. You see, Greg and I had been praying diligently about this decision for months. We knew that God was in control of the destiny of our lives. We knew that if we put our trust in Him, He wouldn't let us down. The natural thing would have been to take matters into our own hands and make a decision. In this way everything would have been settled before I left for Australia. But this didn't enter our heads; God was in control.

It's so much easier to try to take control than to wait for something to happen. Abram and Sarai had been told a baby was on the way, but we can hardly blame them for getting impatient. After all, years had passed and both were really old and past child-producing years. It was not as if they hadn't tried to wait. It's easy in the waiting times to suspect you have "misheard" God or perhaps wonder if there is something you can do to be part of the answer. After all, doesn't God help those who help themselves? But instead of becoming part of the solution, Abram and Sarai became a part of the problem!

Hagar Abused
It was, to say the least, unkind of Hagar's master and mistress to use her as they did, and it had to result in hard feelings. Notice in Genesis 16:2-5 that neither Abram nor Sarai call Hagar by her name! A name is an intensely personal thing. It reminds the world you were special to the

parents who gave you life. It stamps you as an individual with dignity and rights. You can tell how important it is to use someone's personal name by what happens when you forget it!

Since I turned sixty (or even before that), I have had an increasing problem remembering people's names. So many folk feel they "know" you if they have heard you speak, whereas the person who speaks cannot possibly remember the names of everyone who has heard her! People frequently ask, "Jill, do you remember me?" I often do remember faces and tell them so, but that is cold comfort when they want you to remember their names! I am only now learning to say, "I'm sorry, I don't," after spending a lifetime saying hastily, "I-I think I do," or else making up a nice new name for the person. I'm amazed when I do get it right. The pleasure that affords people helps me see how much our personal identities are tied up with our names.

It is very obvious that Abram and Sarai didn't think Hagar's name mattered—at least Sarai didn't. Whenever we verbally abuse someone by addressing that person as "you" or by occupation when we are perfectly aware of his or her name, we are being extremely unkind.

Not only was Hagar treated unkindly, but she was treated unfairly. Life isn't fair, yet one expects some sense of fair play when people know the Lord! It is amazing that Hagar believed in God at all when she was treated so badly by her believing masters. Every so often I meet people who say something like this: "Don't talk to me about Christians. 'So and so' did 'thus and so' to me, and 'they' went to church. So I've never darkened the door of the church again!" It's frightening to realize how we can put people off by not behaving as believers. But it is encouraging that Hagar was able to keep her faith in God separate from her faith in people. That's the secret.

Believers aren't perfect. Maybe some people look to us to be models of perfection, but we all need to remember that at best we are only models of growth and learning. If you find you've been visiting a "quack" doctor, you wouldn't write off the entire medical profession. While I am not at all suggesting Sarai was a "quack" believer, Hagar was apparently astute enough to know her mistress wasn't without faults.

Hagar was undoubtedly a victim of her times. She had been bought as a child slave and sold as merchandise by her own people to a very special family, yes. But then she was used and abused by those who should know better—suffering a double indignity!

Sarai Confused

Now it's Sarai's turn to be illogical! Off she goes to her husband and accuses him of causing the mess! "You are responsible for the wrong I am suffering," she charges (Genesis 16:5), as if Abram caused the maid's disdain!

Abram's feelings about all this are a mystery at this point. He does, however, decline to get involved. "Your servant is in your hands. Do with her whatever you think is best," he says to Sarai in a seemingly offhand manner! (Genesis 16:6).

Sarai took Abram at his word and so mistreated Hagar that the poor girl fled from her (Genesis 16:6). What did Sarai do to Hagar, you may ask? Did she give her a piece of her mind, punish her by silence, or physically take a stick to her? We are not told. The only clue to the nature of the abuse is the word *mistreated*. In the previous chapter, the word is used to describe the sufferings of the entire Hebrew nation in bondage! So whatever Sarai did to Hagar went far beyond a little slap on the wrist! The result was that Hagar fled. Now there weren't too many places to run in the wilderness. It would be a desperate last resort to take your chances out there—especially if you were a pregnant woman and a slave at that! But Hagar, rejected and hurt, ran away anyway.

 **TALK TIME**

1. Choose one of the following to discuss.

   Doesn't God help those who help themselves?

   Why do we find it difficult to wait?

   Whom do you identify with—Abram, Sari, or Hagar—and why?

2. Give an example of someone verbally belittling you. What did you do about it?

 **THINK TIME**

Read the following verses and think about them. All of them have to do with conflict.

Now Abel kept flocks, and Cain worked the soil. In the course of time Cain brought some of the fruits of the soil as an offering to the Lord. But Abel brought fat portions from some of the firstborn of his flock. The Lord looked with favor on Abel and his offering, but on Cain and his offering He did not look with favor. So Cain was very angry. . . .

Then the Lord said to Cain, "Why are you angry? Why is your face downcast? If you do what is right, will you not be accepted? But if you do not do what is right, sin is crouching at your door; it desires to have you, but you must master it."
Now Cain said to his brother Abel, "Let's go out to the field." And while they were in the field, Cain attacked his brother Abel and killed him.
Then the Lord said to Cain, "Where is your brother Abel?"
"I don't know," he replied. "Am I my brother's keeper?" (Genesis 4:2-9)

When the time came for her to give birth, there were twin boys in her womb. The first to come out was red, and his whole body was like a hairy garment; so they named him Esau. After this, his brother came out, with his hand grasping Esau's heel; so he was named Jacob. Isaac was sixty years old when Rebekah gave birth to them.

The boys grew up, and Esau became a skillful hunter, a man of the open country, while Jacob was a quiet man, staying among the tents. Isaac, who had a taste for wild game, loved Esau, but Rebekah loved Jacob. (Genesis 25:24-28)

There was a certain man from Ramathaim, a Zuphite from the hill country of Ephraim, whose name was Elkanah, son of Jeroham, the son of Elihu, the son of Tohu, the son of Zuph, an Ephraimite. He had two wives; one was called Hannah and the other Peninnah. Peninnah had children, but Hannah had none.

Year after year this man went up from his town to worship and sacrifice to the Lord Almighty at Shiloh, where Hophni and Phinehas, the two sons of Eli, were priests of the Lord. Whenever the day came for Elkanah to sacrifice, he would give portions of the meat to his wife Peninnah and to all her sons and daughters. But to Hannah he gave a double portion because he loved her, and the Lord had closed her womb. And because the Lord had closed her womb, her rival kept provoking her in order to irritate her. This went on year after year. Whenever Hannah went up to the house of the Lord, her rival provoked her till she wept and would not eat. Elkanah her husband would say to her, "Hannah, why are you weeping? Why don't you eat? Why are you downhearted? Don't I mean more to you than ten sons?"(1 Samuel 1:1-8)

Write down one thing you think God is saying to you from one of these passages about a conflict in your life.

 **PRAYER TIME**

1. Pray for someone you know who is having infertility problems.

2. Pray about a family conflict (no names).

3. If appropriate, share a personal conflict with a prayer partner. Pray for each other.

4. Pray for people who need patience to wait.

5. Can you think of a relationship where two women are fighting for the attention of one man? Without using names, pray for the situation.

6. Pray about the following concerns.
   Pray for parents who want to adopt.
   Pray for women trying to abort their babies.
   Pray for babies that aren't wanted.

 **ACTION TIME**

Medical Ethics Day
A Christian Perspective

Purpose:
To present a Christian ethic concerning sexuality and related subjects in a way laypeople can understand, so the people in the church might be better equipped to answer the questions of their families, their friends, and their colleagues in the marketplace.

Main sessions:
Can feature qualified speakers on such subjects as euthanasia, abortion, infertility, or AIDS from a Christian perspective. (Use members of the congregation and others in the community as speakers and seminar leaders to avoid undue expense.)

> *Electives could include the following topics*
> Sexuality: What does the Bible say about sex outside of marriage?
> Understanding our sexuality.
> Teaching children about sex.

Related problems, such as PMS and menopause.
Related moral, lega,l and social issues:
How far should a Christian couple go to deal with infertility?
What can "we" do about AIDS?
The legal ramifications of social concern and action concerning abortion.
Caring properly for our elderly parents.

…

CHAPTER THREE
COPING

A Victim of Circumstance
Are you a Hagar? A victim of circumstance? Has someone been unkind and unfair to you? Have you been used or, worse still, abused to such a degree that you have fled from your hurt to some faraway place or some state of mind to escape your misery?

Now this was a desperate and dangerous situation for Hagar. She ran away into the inhospitable, uninhabited, and dry desert. She was pregnant, lonely, and afraid. It isn't too surprising that when the angel of the Lord found her, she was by a well of water. That was a recourse she wasn't expecting. In Genesis 16:8 we read that the angel asked Hagar, "Where have you come from, and where are you going?" Hagar said she was running away from Sarai. After hearing this explanation, the angel told Hagar to go back to her mistress. However, the angel didn't send her back without hope and a sense of security. Hagar was assured that she would have numerous descendants; therefore, Hagar must have realized that her child would be safe if the angel's prophecy was to come true. Also, the angel told Hagar that she should name her unborn child Ishmael which means "God hears." God had heard the crying of the handmaiden in the desert. He wanted Hagar to remember this incident whenever she encountered difficult circumstances. Every time she called her son by his name, she would be reminded of her discussion with the angel of the Lord in the desert. So Hagar returned to Abram and Sarai. She had a son and Abram called the little boy Ishmael.

This is a wonderful example of how you can't run away from your problems; you always take them with you. Or you may be able to run away from your problems for a while, but they always catch up with you. Hagar was in a terrible mess because nobody had been trusting God. However, Hagar could run as far away as she wanted and it would not change the fact that she was pregnant. She was carrying her problems with her.

All of us can remember times when we have tried to run away from our problems. However, when we looked over our shoulders the problems were still there. I heard the story of a great plague in England. This plague was devastating to many communities and multitudes were dying. In fact, a death cart came around in the evenings to collect the corpses. One of the families living in this terrible situation decided to pack their belongings and get out of town while they were still alive. They traveled to a town in the middle of the country that hadn't been touched by the disease. Unfortunately, what this family didn't know was that the plague had contaminated their belongings. Therefore, this family brought the illness with then; and the disease infected the whole town.

This is a graphic example of how running away from difficult circumstances does not make the situation disappear. Everywhere we go, we will take our problems with us, and they may permeate our whole beings. Until we work them out, they will be with us. In fact, if we don't deal with them, we may end up infecting all of those around us.

Do your own methods of coping include running away? You might not physically run away, but there are many ways of escaping while staying in the situation. For example, we may run away through alcohol or drugs, both of which can be used to forget present problems. Or have you ever known people that work all hours of the day and night? If they are busy, then they don't have time to think about their situations. Others may work hard, but if they aren't working, they feel that they must be playing hard. They want to be entertained. They want others around them. They don't want to be left alone for fear of feeling that they have been rejected.

I know someone who couldn't bear to be alone in case he had to think seriously about the issues of life. It wasn't any huge problem or pressing circumstance that pressured him; he just didn't want to think too seriously about the way he was living or the way he was going to die. So he "ran away" by watching TV. In fact, his wife teased him that he watched the screen until the "dot" faded away! Watching soaps, sports, or talk shows can eat up all the quiet moments God gives us to face up to and wrestle with our pressing needs.

Some people run away from their relational problems by leaving people behind and moving on to other relationships. I think one of the many reasons the divorce rate is so high in our society is that many people find it easier to run away from others than face up to their circumstances.

I have a dear friend whose husband left her after years of marriage. She was desolate. There seemed to be no way out of her darkness and despair, and she thought long and hard about taking her life. She talked a little about this "final" way out to a neighbor. After arguing with her, the neighbor said, "If you do decide there's no other way than to take your own life, just remember you'll have to face Jesus and say, 'You weren't enough.'" It was a very sobering thought! My friend decided she'd rather stay and face the mess than face the Master!

For my friend that decision meant a reckoning with certain inevitable facts. Just because you decide to stay and face the mess doesn't mean you find the mess has suddenly disappeared! It's still a mess! The husband won't necessarily come back, or the people involved might not possibly appreciate your grand gesture. It may be a huge effort for you to do the right thing, but you will experience the peace of mind and heart that comes when your conscience is clear and when you know there's nothing more you could have done to put things right. It's really a matter of facing up.

God's Wells

Perhaps the greatest lesson young Hagar learned from her situation was to put her trust in God and not in people! She had learned a little of that already in Abram's tent. Running, frightened, and afraid, she had found herself at a well. What a blessing that was! There were not many wells in the desert. The country was an inhospitable place, and there would in all probability be people around the well that would stare at her and wonder who the strange, young pregnant girl belonged to. Hagar must have felt miserable and apprehensive about her safety. Whom could she trust? She had thought she could trust Abram and Sarai.

It's a dark day when all your people props are knocked out from under you and you are left wondering just what on earth you are going to do! God seems far away, nebulous, unseen, unheard, and even unreal at such times. Except Hagar had just heard His voice! Yes, she had. He had called her by her name and knew she was Sarai's maid. Though He could not be seen, Hagar decided she would give Him a name. He would be called the God who sees! And so Hagar named the place Beer Lahai Roi because, she said, "I have now seen the One who sees me" (Genesis 16:13).

He is indeed the God who looks after the one who looks after Him—the caring, compassionate God who makes wells spring up in our deserts of despair. Though Hagar was used to hearing Abram and Sarai talk of the One True God, she couldn't grasp the huge significance of the fact that she, little Hagar, had heard Him speak to her as clearly as He had spoken to her great master Abram! He was the God of the free and the slave. He was a God who lived to hear, help, and heal people.

We may not hear the voice of God as Hagar heard His voice, of course. She had no Bible to turn to as we do. Let me recommend a well of water called the Word of God to draw from. Not long ago I heard a widow tell of her loneliness and heartache after her husband's very sudden death. Someone had recommended that she read Psalm 54 every morning before facing the new day. She began to do that and started to hear His voice speaking to her situation as clearly as Hagar heard the voice of the Lord in her need.

There are certain passages of Scripture that are particularly helpful for particular problems. We can draw an extra bucket of water from these particular wells at these particular times! For example, the Gideons display such a list in the Bibles they distribute to hotels and other institutions. In case you aren't able to walk into a hotel when trouble comes, the list is displayed at the end of this chapter!

In the good days before trouble comes we need to systematically and regularly absorb "sips of Scripture," storing God's words in our hearts so we can draw on that well when need be. And how do we do that? By using a system of daily readings, such as the Scripture Union Bible guides. Here are some examples of what they offer.

Discovery: a basic Bible guide for mature young people and most adults.

Encounter with God: an advanced Bible guide for church leaders and adults with Bible backgrounds.
Snapshot: a Bible guide for children ages seven to ten.
One up: a Bible study guide for kids eleven to fourteen.

More information may be obtained by contacting Scripture Union, P.O. Box 6720, Wayne, PA 19087 or www.scriptureunion.org. Or you may try out your own method, such as reading a book at a time or a few verses at a sitting. This is the way we hear the voice of God speaking in powerful, relevant terms to our lives! We will find the living God uses His living Word to encourage us into believing in living again!

The discovery that God is a *living* God is a life-changing discovery for all of us. The modern churchgoer may be used to seeing a crucifix in the place of worship. The dead Christ on the cross symbolizes graphically the price of our redemption. But how many of us come into the reality of the living Christ and His life for us and in us? A favorite preacher of mine used to say, "Christ's death makes us fit for heaven, while His life makes us fit for earth!" Christ's living intervention in the midst of our problems makes eternity more than a probability and time once more a possibility. What seemed to be quite impossible now seems to be quite attainable. He lives, and because He lives, He has power to speak to me and act for me.

The second thing Hagar discovered about the Lord as she refreshed herself at the well of water was that He *loves*. Only a loving God would lead her to a well in a desert! Only a loving God would so guide her life that she should become Abram and Sarai's servant. Hard though her life had been, Hagar must have realized she would never have made these vital discoveries about God if she had not spent years with these people who knew Him. Certainly her own people, the Egyptians, knew no such things about such a living, loving, eternal being.

One of the hardest things to realize is that God loves you. We perhaps come to an intellectual acknowledgment of the fact, but the *heart* knowledge isn't there. We don't "feel" loved—whatever that feels like! Perhaps we are expecting some parallel sensation that we experience when someone human loves us, a sense that responds to some stimulus or other. The Bible doesn't tell us what it feels like to love God, but it does tell us to do it. It also tells us God loves us and demonstrated it by doing things for us: things like leaving heaven; being born a baby;

being rejected, tortured, and murdered; being buried "our" way; in one of "our" graves, in one of "our" cities, on one of "our" days! I don't know what He felt toward us, but I do know He could do all that only because He loved us.

We all know actions speak louder than words. Hagar knew God loved her because of the well of water. Who had guided her wandering steps in unknown terrain? She knew it because of the life stirring within her. Only a mother knows that incredible confirmation of His grace and giving! And she knew of God's love because she found the courage somewhere, somehow to turn her heart toward home!

Third, Hagar came to understand that God *listens*. Had He not listened to her desperate prayers for water in the burning heat? If she had any doubts as to this aspect of His character, all she needed to do was think about the name of her baby Ishmael and what it meant: "God hears" (Genesis 16:11). In the years to come, as she submitted herself to Sarai and served her under the uneasy truce the two women would work out together, there would be many a time Hagar would call to Ishmael and immediately be reminded of

God's listening ear. Who does not need to know that? "If only I had someone to listen to me," sighs the lonely and dejected widower. "You never listen to me," complains the

young child competing with his siblings for his mother's ears. "Nobody cares about my opinions," gripes the teenager battling for attention. Let me tell you with great joy—there is One who listens. He is never "dull of hearing" and His ear is tuned to the poor and troubled. He listens to the cry of those in cruel places (Exodus 3:7), and He listens to the heartbeat of the elderly and sick. They are heard; assuredly, they are heard! Remember, God is your friend and He listens.

It took a terrible row and severe punishment to bring about the circumstances that led Hagar to discover that God lives and loves and listens. Having learned those lessons, she must have felt she could cope with the rest of the story! When we don't or won't listen to God, sometimes He has to use a megaphone!

I think of the strange pain in my stomach that took me into hospital while a student at college. Perhaps there was no other way I could have met the young nurse who herself was ill and in the bed beside me. It was she who led me to Christ. I discovered the eternal well of water in a desert of sickness. It was through a girl—not an angel—that I heard for the first time that God lives and loves and listens. I believed and went back to a difficult world, teaching children who came from deprived backgrounds in Liverpool the same truths I had discovered for myself in hospital.

He helped me face up to reality instead of living in a fantasy world. Accepting something I couldn't change (my illness) was the first thing I had to do, and then I could set about changing the things I could, such as the lives of the kids I was teaching. His life filled me, His love flowed through me, and I listened to the One who listened to me!

Facing up isn't easy. It wasn't easy for Hagar and it won't be easy for us. Here are one or two pointers that might help. We are not in a position to know too much about the steps Hagar took to reconcile with Sarai. All we know is that she went home. Something was undoubtedly said. Words were used to bridge the cold hostility. Maybe Sarai had been feeling guilty about it all and maybe she hadn't; we just don't know. So what do we deduce about the first step to reconciliation? Someone has to take the first step and it doesn't need to be the guilty party.

Owning Your Part of the Problem
If Hagar owned her part of the problem first, that certainly would have helped. Perhaps she had time to think about it as she retraced her steps. It's always a good idea to own something, and there will always be something to own. It may be a very little something, or it may be a great, big something. Whatever the problem may be, it takes two to quarrel.

Hagar could have owned her part of the problem by expressing how sorry she was about despising her mistress for her infertility. That's when the trouble between the two women really began in earnest, if you remember (Genesis 16:4). Maybe Sarai said she was sorry she had taken advantage of her privileged position and had treated Hagar so badly. I'd like to think that that was the case and that she spoke first. Reconciliation comes a lot easier if the first words heard are not accusatory! It's the easiest thing in the world to want the other person to be the first to own the fault.

I remember feeling hurt because my husband had forgotten my birthday. It was just a little thing; but because we didn't talk about it, it grew quickly into a very big thing. I began to almost believe he had done it deliberately! How silly that was. I decided I would let him know by my pained expression that something was wrong but would make him guess exactly what it was. Of course, that was pretty impossible without even a hint. When he didn't guess, that made me angrier than ever!

After a while I began to realize how childish I was. I decided to have it out and get it over with. I knew I should own my part, but I couldn't think of one thing I should own! I couldn't help having birthdays. After all, everyone had them whether he or she wanted to or not, and it shouldn't be too hard to remember them since they happened with monotonous regularity!

Then I suddenly thought of something. I had forgotten our wedding anniversary that year, and he had remembered it! There now, I could own that. That was just as bad as, if not worse than, forgetting a birthday! So I was able to say something like this: "Stuart, I've been really hurt because you forgot my birthday, but I've just remembered I forgot our wedding anniversary, so I know how hard it can be when we are both so busy! Why don't we drop our plans for the evening, and you can take me out for a meal to celebrate!" It did the trick, and instead of enjoying a pout I enjoyed a lovely meal with my husband.

Now that was a very minor thing to get upset about, but it doesn't take much to fan a spark into a blaze. If we try hard enough, we can find one thing on our side to use as a plank to build a bridge across the yawning gap between us. So the first part of facing up to the things that have to be faced is to find some fault you can call your own in the whole situation. Use that to open the lines of communication. In other words, decide to speak first.

Accepting Things You Cannot Change
The second aspect of facing up is to look the facts in the face and accept the things you cannot change. God helped Hagar to do just that. He reminded her that He cared for her and then gently helped her to face reality. "Hagar, Sarai's servant," He called to her from heaven (Genesis 16:8). It must have been a strange sound in her ears! Remember, Sarai had avoided using Hagar's name altogether, which was not a bit kind or loving. The Lord, however, called her by name, a fact that told the poor, rejected girl God saw her plight and cared about her personally.

Hard on the heels of her name, however, came the stark reminder that she was indeed Sarai's servant! That's after all how it was, and it was no good pretending anything else. But He knew; yes, He knew! His personal concern with our personal concerns transcends the cold, impersonal attitudes of others around us! Someone cares! It's easy in moments of dire emotional distress like Hagar's to believe no one cares at all. Hagar must have been tempted to wonder that, if she didn't matter to Sarai, then did she matter to anyone else in the world? "But how do we *know* He cares?" you may ask. When others don't care, and we've become the victim of our circumstances, how can we even begin to believe God cares for us? Surely if He did, He would have intervened on our behalf. I believe in the revelation of Scripture. I believe Jesus Christ is God. Believing this leads me to watch Him as He heals and helps, touches the untouchables and bends the unbendable. I hear Him calling out the personal names of His disciples as He calls them to leave their nets and follow Him. He speaks up for victims and became one Himself in order to bear our griefs and carry our sorrows. His enemies refused to use His God-given name, choosing to ridicule and insult Him instead, and in the end they cast Him out and crucified Him. He thoroughly understands the Hagars among us.

He also faced reality, giving us a model to follow. When things got tough for Jesus, He was reminded of His role as servant and of His need to submit to the will of the Father even though He was being mistreated. Jesus was able to accept the things He couldn't change and say, "Not My will but Thine be done" (Matthew 26:39). Facing up to the crisis means owning a part of the problem and, if possible, taking the initiative toward reconciliation. Then face reality, accept the things you cannot change, and remind yourself meanwhile of God's personal concern with your life and the model He left for us to emulate.

Cautions

Let me state loudly and clearly, I am not saying to allow yourself to be abused! When Hagar went back to Sarai, it was with the assurance that God would take care of the mistreatment. How do I know that? Because He told her the baby would be all right. He talked with Hagar about her descendants (Genesis 16:10)! The Bible doesn't tell us to submit to any old thing, but it's full of examples of people who by the giving grace of God make the best of bad marriages, uncomfortable relationships, and trying circumstances. Let me say it again: God assured Hagar He had a plan in mind for her and her child. Unpleasant though it might be, the safest and best place to raise her baby was in Abram's tent! So we need to submit if possible to the people God has given to care for us, unless *there is danger of a very real kind.*

For example, if there is a physical and/or emotional danger to yourself and/or your children, then there is no point in going back. In these circumstances, returning may cause more problems. Instead, you should go to your church or a recommended professional service and ask for some guidance as to what you should do.

In high school and college, I was jealous of my two brothers because they didn't worry about their grades though they were both good students. Getting top grades just wasn't one of their top three or four priorities. This is where we differed. I wanted top grades. Not only did I want these grades, but I studied and overstudied to such a degree that I was almost guaranteed of getting these grades. Unfortunately, sometimes this made the rest of my life rather miserable. I was so anxious about my grades that I couldn't enjoy other things.

During one of my college breaks, I had a long talk with Mom about this I told her that if only I was like David or Peter, then everything would be all right. I can still remember the advice that she gave to me. She said that I would never be like my brothers. We are very different. Probably I would always strive for the top grades; however, there was nothing necessarily wrong with this approach to life. What was wrong was the way I went about it I would have to learn to deal with my anxiety and drive. I couldn't go through life always feeling this way.

This was good advice. I was to try to change what I could change; that is, my approach to everything. In doing so I would learn to deal with what I couldn't change.

When I moved to New York City, I was amazed at the examples of wealth and poverty existing side by side. Night after night I saw homeless people lying on the cold concrete ground to get a few hours of fitful sleep. I felt so helpless forever thinking that there had to be something I could do. Yet how can one person improve this whole situation? Obviously, one person couldn't solve such a huge problem. I realized that some things were simply out of my control yet there are other things that I could do.

Over the years I have tried to help in tiny ways. For example, a close friend, who is a social worker, and I helped set up a committee in our church to adopt a homeless family. Now this didn't resolve the plight of the homeless in general, but at least our church is trying to get involved and help in a small way. We all need to think of ways to get involved.

After facing up to God, giving control to God, and submitting ourselves to Him and the people in the situation, we will need to continue to look up to God for the rest of our lives! Through a crisis Hagar learned to face up, give up, and look up to God. Now the process began. As she turned her steps toward home, she learned to lean on God. The last stretch of this journey must have been the hardest.

In my senior year of high school I ran on the cross-country team. Unfortunately, I joined only a few days before the first meet and didn't have time to build up my stamina. My first meet was also one of the biggest meets of the season, taking place on a hot day with temperatures in the high 90s.

Coming to the stretch marking the last quarter mile of the track I felt as if my body had died. I was totally exhausted from running so fast and could barely keep going because of the intense heat. The coach started yelling to me to pick up my pace. You see, in cross-country racing the first five team members to finish the race count for the team victory, and I was the fifth runner. For our team to stand a chance of winning I had to keep going and pass a few people

Well, I didn't think I could go any farther. I remember saying something to my coach about quitting. At that point he started jogging beside me, pacing me, and encouraging me to give it one last kick. You wouldn't believe the difference his encouragement made! All of a sudden I was able to muster up some energy and determination to finish the race. I don't know where it came from because I was literally ready to drop, but I was able to keep going. Our team won the meet.

Many of our problems are like this race; it is the last stretch that is the hardest. However, we need to realize that God is in control of every situation of our lives. He is our own personal coach who will run alongside us and shower us with words of encouragement during the most intense periods. Then we can run that last stretch. With God as our coach, we can keep going and face whatever is ahead.

TALK TIME

1. Use the following as discussion starters.

   What are your problems?

   How do you run away from your problems?

   Think of an example of a conflict in your life that you took the initiative to resolve. How did the conflict work out?

   Share a verse that has helped you with a particular problem.

   Share an experience when God has been your coach during the last stretch of the race to the finish line.

   Share a system of Bible reading you have found helpful (a few minutes each).

2. Look up the following verses and see what the Word of God says about itself.

   Psalm 119:105
   Matthew 4:4
   Hebrews 4:12
   1 Peter 1:25

3. You can know God loves you too—for all the above reasons and more. Make a list of all the ways God has been good to you and your family. "Count your many blessings," as the hymn has it, "name them one by one, and it will surprise you what the Lord hath done."

THINK TIME

Pick the references that are relevant to your needs. Look up, read, and meditate on them. (This list was compiled by the Gideon Bible Society.)

Where to Find Help When Afraid:
  Psalm 34:4
  Matthew 10:28
  2 Timothy 1:7
  Hebrews 13:5-6
Where to Find Help When Anxious:
  Psalm 46
  Matthew 6:19-34
  Philippians 4:6
  1 Peter 5:6-7
Where to Find Help When Backsliding:
  Psalm 51
  1 John 1:4-9
Where to Find Help When Bereaved:
  Matthew 5:4
  2 Corinthians 1:3-4
Where to Find Help When Bitter or Critical:
  1 Corinthians 13
Where to Find Help When Conscious of Sin:
  Proverbs 28:13
Where to Find Help When Defeated:
  Romans 8:31-39
Where to Find Help When Depressed:
  Psalm 34
Where to Find Help When Disaster Threatens:
  Psalm 91
  Psalm 118:5-6
  Luke 8:22-25
Where to Find Help When Discouraged:
  Psalm 23
  Psalm 42:6-11
  Psalm 55:22
  Matthew 5:11-12
  2 Corinthians 4:8-18
Philippians 4:4-7

John 16:33
  Where to Find Help When Doubting:

Matthew 8:26
Hebrews 11
Where to Find Help When Facing a Crisis:
Psalm 121
Matthew 6:25-34
Hebrews 4:16
Where to Find Help When Faith Fails:
Psalm 42:5
Hebrews 11
Where to Find Help When Friends Fail:
Psalm 41:9-13
Luke 17:3-4
Romans 12:14, 17, 19, 21
2 Timothy 4:16-18
Where to Find Help When Leaving Home:
Psalm 121
Matthew 10:16-20
Where to Find Help When Lonely:
Psalm 23
Hebrews 13:5-6
Where to Find Help When Needing God's Protection:
Psalm 27:1-6
Psalm 91
Philippians 4:19
Where to Find Help When Needing Guidance:
Psalm 32:8
Proverbs 3:5-6
Where to Find Help When Needing Peace:
John 14:1-4
John 16:33
Romans 5:1-5
Philippians 4:6-7
Where to Find Help When Needing Rules for Living:
Romans 12
Where to Find Help When You Need to Overcome:
Psalm 6
Romans 8:31-39
1 John 1:4-9

Where to Find Help When Prayerful:
  Psalm 4
  Psalm 42
  Luke 11:1-13
  John 17
  1 John 5:14-15
Where to Find Help When Needing Protection:
  Psalm 18:1-3
  Psalm 34:7
Where to Find Help When Sick or in Pain:
  Psalm 38
  James 5:14-15
  Romans 8:28, 38-39
  2 Corinthians 12:9-10,13,19
Where to Find Help When Sorrowful:
  Psalm 51
  Matthew 5:4
  John 14
  2 Corinthians 1:3-4
  1 Thessalonians 4:13-18
Where to Find Help When Tempted:
  Psalm 1
  Psalm 139:23-24
  Matthew 26:41
  1 Corinthians 10:12-14
  Philippians 4:8
  James 4:7
  2 Peter 2:9
  2 Peter 3:17
Where to Find Help When Thankful:
  Psalm 100
  1 Thessalonians 5:18
  Hebrews 13:15
Where to Find Help When Traveling:
  Psalm 121
Where to Find Help When in Trouble:
  Psalm 16
  Psalm 31

John 14:1-4
Hebrews 7:25
Where to Find Help When Weary:
Psalm 90
Matthew 11:28-30
1 Corinthians 15:58
Galatians 6:9-10
Where to Find Help When Worried:
Matthew 6:19-34
1 Peter 5:6-7

PRAYER TIME

1. Take time to pray about the following concerns.

    Pray for someone who's running away from his or her problems.
    Pray for those going back to face difficult circumstances.
    Pray for people in dangerous domestic situations.
    Pray for counselors and people helpers.
    Pray for those people who are teaching others how to draw water from the wells of the Word of God.

2. Make a daily prayer list. Each day, pray for someone like Hagar.

    Sunday:

    Monday:

    Tuesday:

    Wednesday:

    Thursday:

    Friday:

    Saturday:

ACTION TIME

Purpose:
A church may be able to help those teenagers in the community who feel that they have no one to go to with their problems.

Action Ideas:
Crisis help line for teenagers who need help.
Counseling services that are open to kids in the community.
Big Brother or Big Sister program for kids who are in trouble.

Crisis help line:
  A. Objectives
     1. Help teenagers know that there are people who really care for them.
        Help teenagers to see how much God loves them through our behavior and attitudes.

  B. Areas to cover
     1. Room or rooms to set up telephones
     2. Telephones
     3. Volunteers to answer the phones
     4. Places for the teens to come to
     5. Others _____

  C. Specific procedure
     1. Speak with the church leadership and determine if this action is appropriate for your church.
     2. Decide who will pray for, organize, and implement the program.
     3. Get in touch with local social service agencies or other churches that have already implemented these programs and ask them to help you get started.
     4. Decide how to arouse the awareness and interest of the church in the project so that people will volunteer to help.
        Provide speakers on certain topics, such as teenage pregnancy, drug use, etc.
        Show videos on these different topics.

5. Get enough volunteers so that a few people aren't carrying the whole burden. If you don't do this, those few who volunteer will burn out quickly.
6. Train the volunteers. Get help from social service agencies or other churches who have implemented similar programs.
7. Decide how to advertise to the community that this service is available.
   a) Fliers
   b) Advertising in the local paper
   c) Posters in the public schools or places where kids usually "hang out"

CHAPTER FOUR
COMMUNITY

The New Hagar
With God walking alongside her, Hagar returned to Abram and Sarai. Then Ishmael was born. We can't be sure about all the family dynamics but we do know that Hagar stayed about fifteen years. Therefore, the two women must have reached some sort of agreement.

There is no doubt in my mind that Hagar discovered the power to be different in her human relationships because of her new understanding of the living God who lived and loved and listened to her. Feeling cared for on the inside *has to help you care for those on the* outside *of your life.*

Shortly after I came to understand that God cared for me, the loneliness I had experienced was filled up with the personal presence of God. Now I knew He loved me! It was not as if I had been unloved or uncared for by my family, but when God lives within the human heart, He brings such satisfaction that it is possible to turn your focus outward to share with others the help you are receiving.

As a young school teacher in Liverpool, I volunteered to get involved with teenagers after school hours. To teach math, English, drama, and art all day is well and good, but when God has become your friend, that needs to be taught as well. When I began to care for the people who lived on the outside of my life, I discovered, like Hagar, the youngsters didn't always respond to my "grand gestures" of unselfishness. Yet it was enough that I tried in God's strength to care for those who didn't particularly care for me!

Within my family things were different too because I was different. I was a "new" Jill in the old family. The folks didn't always appreciate the newness, or so they said, but I found a strength I never had before to try to make a difference in my home situation. Before I knew the Lord, I would never volunteer to help around the house. I would wait to be volunteered by my father or mother. "Go and help your mother, Jill," was a "constant" from my father. At this directive, I would sigh from my boots, drag myself out of my chair, and slowly and sulkily comply. Usually my mother would take one look at my face and decline my offer! Now though, new in Christ, I found a desire to serve cheerfully. I determined my father would not have to "command" me to be helpful anymore. Now *that* made quite an impression on my parents! I learned to serve for the first time in my life—not for reward, but just because I loved Him and loved them. It wasn't easy, but it was so worthwhile.

It certainly would not have been easy for Hagar to return and face the music different person though she was! Because we have the benefit of hindsight and the Bible, we know that Sarai and Abram would accept their runaway servant back again, but Hagar certainly didn't know that. She went back in obedience and faith, having no idea whether or not she would be accepted. It would be in the strength He gave her—not in her own—that she would return to show her masters the "new" Hagar.

In addition to the strength God gives, another resource we should consider *is the family.* Everybody has a family structure. It may not be a traditional family or a happy family, but everyone has someone they call "family." Even Hagar had a family. Her family structure consisted of Abram and Sarai and her fellow servants. Ishmael, her own son, was soon to join her family too. Some of these people in the circle around her were kind and some were unkind. It was not an ideal family, but in Hagar's society this was the only family that she had.

God intended the family to be a warm womb to nourish and cherish those within the comforting circumference of its environment. The Bible says God put the solitary man Adam in a family because He knew that it "was not good for the man to be alone" (Genesis 2:18).

Humans are not islands; we cannot exist in splendid isolation. Human beings need each other. Abram needed Sarai and Sarai needed Abram. Sarai and Abram needed Hagar and vice versa. Ishmael needed them all. In fulfilling each other's needs, we fulfill our own. We find value in being valued. We mature as we practice working out our differences together. Selfishness shows up quickly under the family magnifying glass and can be dealt with quickly if the family is functioning as it should.

Of course, that is the key—*as it should*. If the family isn't functioning, then *all* the family members are in trouble. This is good because all should feel some responsibility for keeping the peace or mending the breaches in the family walls!

Although many in our society believe that there is not an answer for how families can be rebuilt, we believe differently. The Christian believes that the love of God can begin to hold the family together. Love—God's love—comes into our homes when He comes into our hearts.

God's type of love means that you are primarily concerned with someone else's well-being, irrespective of the cost to yourself. It is an altruistic, unchangeable, inexhaustible love. You will give and keep on giving without ever expecting anything in return. This is a hard type of love for us to conceive of in our society. It seems that people may be willing to give love, but they expect something in return.

Obviously, this type of love isn't easy to demonstrate. Therefore, it has to be a love of action *and not* emotion. *We can all think of times when we should have shown someone love yet we didn't because we really didn't* feel *like it. God says that we should love others even when we don't feel like it.*

The Greek word for this type of love is agape, *and the Bible is filled with examples of it. God demonstrated agape love when He created the earth and put us on it. His most meaningful demonstration of agape love was when He sent His one and only Son to die at Calvary. I have three sons. I don't think I would be able to give up any one of my sons for someone else. God had only one Son, and He was crucified on Calvary for our sins.*

When my mom is reading the Bible, she likes to "peek around the corner of a verse." We can try this with the story of Barabbas, the murderer who was supposed to die at Calvary. Instead, when Pontius Pilate asked the people who they wanted to have released, they yelled for Barabbas to be set free and Jesus to be crucified. What do you think Barbados did when he was let out of the jail cell? Do you think he followed the throngs of people toward Calvary? Do you think he wondered who was being crucified on his cross? Do you think he went up to John or one of the women at the foot of the cross and asked them who had taken his place? If he had done these things, the person who responded would have told him that the man on the cross was Jesus, the Son of God. If Barbados had asked what Jesus had done wrong, the answer would have been "nothing." Though this might have seemed extremely difficult to believe, one fact would have been certain. Jesus was on the cross instead of Barabbas, Jesus was taking Barabbas' place, Jesus was paying the price for Barabbas' mistakes, Jesus the Son of God was suffering unimaginable pain and sorrow so that Barabbas, a common criminal, could have another chance at life. This is what is meant when we speak of agape love.

God helps us love the unlovely, the quick tempered, the unkind, and the untrue. He drives us to right the wrongs, say we are sorry, and make amends. Love *is always* busy, bustling about the Lord's business, whistling a merry tune of joy and reconciliation and hope; He is sure of His ability to grow love if we will only give Him half a chance.

So it needs to begin with us! We cannot leave it to Abram, or Sarai, or anyone else. We are responsible for *our* part in it all. Hagar, as far as we know, did *her* bit and that is all God asked of her. It is all He asks of us! However, we have to ask Him to supply us with agape love because the other types of love described in the Bible are not enough.

Looking at our society today we can see that human love and the sexual aspect of love are not always enough to keep people together. First phileo, *or human love, is the type of love that a mother has for a child, a brother for a sister, a husband for a wife, or two friends for each other. It is a need love as opposed to a gift love. We all need to be needed, so it is only natural for us to want phileo love. However, we should keep in mind that our natural loves must not rival our love for God. They must be submitted to agape's control.*

Finally, there is eros *love. This word is used to describe the sensual, physical aspect of love—the feeling that is too big for words. Eros is passionate, romantic, and sentimental; however it is also changeable, egotistical, and limited. C.S. Lewis once said, "Eros is always driven to promise sincerely what Eros himself is powerless to perform." This is a mouthful, so let me give you an example. When my younger brother was about fifteen, he "fell in love." He was starry-eyed for days and then his mood suddenly changed. One night Pete said to my mom, "She promised to love me always, and now she says that she doesn't love me anymore." This shows how changeable eros love can be.*

Our world today worships eros love instead of agape love. We hear it on the radio and we see it on the TV. The statement is loud and clear: if it feels good then it must be right. Now I am not saying that eros love wasn't created by God. In fact, He created this type of love along with agape and phileo. However, He created this type of love to be subjected to His commands. We must obey what God tells us to do and not what eros love tells us to do.

Perhaps you have been a little shocked at a new aspect of Abram and Sarai's character that we have looked at in this book. Maybe you have revered them both because of all the great things you have read about them in other parts of the Scriptures, for example in Romans 4 and Hebrews 11:8-19. Even Sarai is given a badge of honor there, and is also held up as an example in 1 Peter 3:6. Peter tells all women they should behave as Sarah did in respect to their husbands and develop a responsive spirit. But we know, don't we, that though she treated Abram with respect, she didn't do too well when it came to treating her handmaiden properly!

No family is perfect; all leave something to be desired. The reason for this glaring inconsistency in the lives of many who profess to know God is something the Bible calls *carnality*. A few definitions may help.

A *natural* person, according to the Scriptures, is someone without the Spirit of God. In fact, the Bible goes so far as to say, "If anyone does not have the Spirit of Christ, he does not belong to Christ" (Romans 8:9). The *natural* person lives his life with *self* as his focus.

The *spiritual* person is someone who has had a chance to understand the nature of God as holy, his or her own fallen nature, and the gracious offer of God's forgiveness. The spiritual person has invited God within and has been ignited or spiritually illuminated from that point on to understand spiritual things. "We know also that the Son of God has come and has given us understanding, so that we may know him who is true. And we are in him who is true—even in his Son Jesus Christ. He is the true God and eternal life" (1 John 5:20). The spiritual person now knows what the Lord God requires of him, and tries to live and love accordingly.

The *carnal* person is one who was a natural person, has become a spiritual person, but is choosing to live like a natural one! Any Christian can do this. The choice comes daily to "live after the Spirit and His principles or after the flesh (self) and its whims!" (Romans 8:13, author's paraphrase).

Sarai had much against her. She had neither Bible, church, nor the letters of the Apostle Paul in her hand. She, like us, was far from perfect. Many times, like us, she lived "after the flesh, and not after the Spirit." The problem is that when we do that, other Christians may understand and forgive us for it, but the Hagars and Ishmaels of this world may not!

How does the teenager grapple with the inconsistency of a parent singing hymns by his side in church yet bawling him out over lunch? Or what does a husband do with a wife who spends hours "counseling" other women on the phone, but who hardly speaks to him all evening? Or what about the man who holds office in the church, but flirts openly with his female employees or neglects the smallest of his home responsibilities? Can these sorts of families possibly be a resource for their members? I believe the answer is yes! Families, as God intended them to be, have an awful lot to offer in the way of a support system for the individuals that live within their boundaries. The family is a good idea because it gives us a chance to understand what community is about and gives us opportunities to give and take.

TALK TIME

1. Discuss the following.
   Whom do you consider your family? (Share photos!)
   How is love shown in your family?
2. How has your experience of God caring for you on the inside of your life helped you to care for people on the outside of your life? Give an example.

3. Why do you think people who are great Christians sometimes act in unchristian ways?

4. Discuss the phrase: "It [love] needs to begin with us." Do you agree?

THINK TIME

1. Read Romans 7:14—8:11.

2. Make two lists of the things Paul says are spiritual and the things that are carnal.

3. Think about the following:
   How does being spiritual affect home life?
   Give an example.

   How does being carnal affect home life?
   Give an example.

4. Commit to memory a verse from this passage that has helped you.

PRAYER TIME

1. Pray for intact families to be strengthened. Pray for help for fractured families. Pray for the church's role in helping all families.

2. Think quietly about *one* area of your life that needs to be different. Pray about it.

3. Does your family know you are a "new" person because of your relationship to Christ?
If your answer is no, what specific action can you take to show them?

4. Pray for the "old" family to notice the "new" you. If all your family members know God, pray for families around you who don't.

5. Pray for Christian families who are spiritual, but living as though they were natural. No names.

ACTION TIME

Purpose:
Establish ministries for single parents.

Action ideas for spiritual growth:
1. Bible study groups for the following people.
   Widowed parents
   Divorced parents (parents with or without custody of children)
   Separated parents (parents with or without custody of children)
   Single parents

2. One-on-one discipleship programs using NavPress or Campus Crusade materials for the groups of single parents listed above.

   NavPress
   P.O. Box 35001
   Colorado Springs, CO 80935

   Campus Crusade
   New Life Publications
   100 Sunport Lane
   Orlando, FL 32809

3. Sunday School studies that meet the needs of the single parent (e.g., Hagar and Ishmael, widow of Nain).

4. Prayer chain among single parents.

   Action ideas for social family activities: (These can include either single-parent families or a combination of two-parent families and single-parent families.)

   1. Activities related to holiday times.
      Thanksgiving dinner
      Cut-your-own-Christmas-tree party
      Attend fireworks on Fourth of July

   2. Roller skating, ice skating, bowling, etc.
   3. Family sports night (Use YMCA or school facilities if a church gym is not available.)

4. Drama groups, "family" and otherwise

5. Picnics in parks in the summer

6. Visits to local events together (e.g., state fairs, amusement parks, circus)

7. Potlucks

8. VCR nights (family films)

Service projects (projects that churches could implement to help the single-parent family):

1. Food pantry at the church

2. Seminars and workshops for parents and children
Biblical seminars
Practical workshops for women faced with the "traditional" men's jobs at home
(e.g., plumbing, fixing the car, finances)

3. Moving committee
Help those who don't have the money to move themselves
Help those who don't have the "muscle" to move themselves

4. Child care

5. Whole families who could "adopt" a single-parent family

6. Men and women who can befriend children from single-parent homes

7. Christmas party for the children of single parents

CHAPTER FIVE
CHANGE

Change in the Family

One of the exciting things about the family is that it is never static. It is ever-changing with the seasons of life. Hagar and her son had no idea that an event was about to take place that would alter their family relationships forever. The huge event we are talking about, of course, is the birth of Isaac. Any new arrival in the life of a family causes incredible demand for adjustment on everyone's behalf.

I have a friend who told me that after the new baby was brought home from the hospital, the older sister received the "intruder" well and seemed to be responding lovingly. After a brief week, however, the little girl suggested to her mother that the baby had stayed long enough and she could return it to the hospital! I'm sure Ishmael could relate to that!

When Ishmael was thirteen years old God appeared to Abram. He told Abram that He was still going to fulfill His covenant through him. Abram's name would be changed to Abraham, "the father of many nations." As a sign of the promise God made with Abram, every man had to be circumcised. God also told Abram that Sarai would have a part in this plan. Her name would be changed to Sarah, which means "Princess."

Well, at this point Abraham fell facedown and laughed. You see, he was ninety-nine years old and Sarah was about eighty-nine. I guess it would be a little hard for someone in our day to imagine an eighty-nine-year-old woman getting pregnant. Considering the situation carefully, Abraham realized that he already had a son. He asked God if the covenant could be fulfilled through Ishmael. God said that Ishmael would be included in the blessings. He would be the father of twelve rulers. However, the covenant would be fulfilled through a child that would be born to Sarah.

After his conversation with God, Abraham took all the males in his household including Ishmael, and circumcised them. By including Ishmael in this act Abraham was saying that his son would be blessed. God would take care of this young boy. Ishmael had not asked to be put into this situation. He couldn't help the way things had turned out. This is a good lesson for all of us. Sometimes we find ourselves in situations that we didn't ask to be placed into. In fact, we don't really want to be in these situations. Yet if we are doing what God wants us to do, He will take care of us. He will bless us in the same way that He blessed Ishmael.

Despite everyone's doubting, Sarah had a son. She and Abraham called him Isaac. When Isaac was two or three, he was weaned, and Abraham threw a huge party to celebrate this major event in his son's life (Genesis 21:8). If you turn back a few pages of your Bible, you will not find any indication that Ishmael had a party when he was weaned. Therefore, when we read in Genesis 21 that during Isaac's party, Ishmael "mocks" his baby brother, we shouldn't be too surprised. I would think that Ishmael was very hurt that his baby brother was getting something special. Ishmael may have felt abandoned and rejected. In order to get back at his brother, he decided to mock him. The word mock *is the same word used in Galatians 4:29. It means to persecute or torment. This was more than the ordinary bickering that goes on between siblings.*

Which of us cannot relate to this? In some measure, all of us who have brothers or sisters can think back to situations where siblings were honored, favored, or noticed when we were not. I can remember at Ishmael's age being "tennis mad." All my spare time was taken up with practicing, playing, and competing. My older sister played too. One day my parents put on a tennis day at our home's backyard court for all her friends. A tournament schedule was organized, lunch was prepared, and a party closed the day. I can still remember feeling left out. I became very angry and hostile and refused to join in. Why had *she* been given the tennis party and not me? It wasn't fair. I threw a tantrum and

caused as much trauma as I could. This way, by spoiling my sister's party, I could get back at her. I was selfish and silly, yes—spoiled and riled, certainly—but I surely could relate to Ishmael! And think of it— he was the *older* and his tiny brother was the one being fussed over!

In our family, though my parents worked so hard to make sure everything was evenly distributed between my brothers and me, there were times when we didn't feel that things were "fair." One day my older brother David and I marched my younger brother Peter in to see my mother. We told her there was something terribly wrong with Peter. At first Mom was a little alarmed. David and I looked so serious, and Peter had guilt written all over his small face. "Whatever is the matter?" she asked. In all seriousness we told her that Peter actually thought he was as important as us. We informed her that this wasn't possible because David was number one, I was number two, and Peter was number three. Therefore, how could he possibly be as important as either David or me?

On another occasion I can remember very clearly thinking that my parents had not been fair to me. I came home from college to visit for the weekend. On Saturday afternoon Peter hurried through the kitchen, muttering that he wouldn't be home for dinner because he had a date. I casually inquired about his curfew and found out it was a lot later than mine had been at his age. I raised my objection, but it didn't seem to do any good. I remember thinking that I must have broken a lot of ground so my younger brother could have such an easy ride!

I recollect I spent two wonderful days with my grandchildren, and I was reminded that people can be supersensitive to favoritism. I returned with photos, anecdotes, glowing reports, stories, and funny things my husband just had to hear about the boys' every move, word, and burp! After some considerable time amid the happy flow of words, my husband said; "I have a feeling other members of this family have just slid off the world into oblivion!" We laughed together! I knew it was all right, but I did take note to take care I didn't give the impression that *any* one child or grandchild, or parent, was any more or less important than the other.

When these situations arise in families, it's easy to take out your frustrations on whomever happens to be around.

Modeling
Ishmael may have learned to mock by modeling after his mother. He may have been imitating her attitude and her actions. In Genesis 16:5 we saw that when Hagar found out she was pregnant, she despised and

mocked her mistress. Though this occurred before Ishmael was born, there may have been some underlying tensions within the household during the first fifteen years of Ishmael's life. Considering the circumstances, this would not have been surprising! Children can pick up attitudes very easily.

How easy it is to blame other people for our bad temper or our bad moods, especially our children. It is pretty common to hear a young, harassed mother complaining that her children have been driving her crazy. It is my own experience that children don't *create* your attitude—they *reveal* it! When jogged, a cup full of sweet water cannot spill one bitter drop. People may jog our emotions during the course of a day, and what fills our lives is what spills out of our lives. I heartily sympathize with the single young mother of three small children understandably exhausted by the children's bedtime. "Why do you always say 'Thank goodness' instead of saying 'Good night'?" inquired a little one. Why indeed!

When my husband was on the road for long periods of time during the course of his work, I used to get pretty down. It was tiring work dealing with three preschoolers. I would battle with resentment against his job, the people who sent him away on these trips, and even with God Himself for allowing it all to happen! Whenever I would nurture these negative feelings until they filled my life, the children picked them up. I was making a serious effort to hide them, but it would take only a fight between the children or a sudden crisis demanding extra effort on my part to "jog" the cup of my raw emotions and out would spill the angry word, the impatient put-down, or a nasty remark. It didn't take much time after that to blame the children for my bad temper! "They would drive anyone to distraction," I complained to a friend.

The next step was a foregone conclusion. The children, "splashed" with the bitter water overflowing from my life, began to complain too! They started resenting their father's absence, whining about everything and everybody. It didn't take long to realize what was happening! My job was to stay full of the Spirit so that when jogged, I could reveal just what it was that filled my life and not allow the children to pick up my negative attitudes. The difference was truly astounding. Prayers were prayed for Daddy and his work for the Lord—and for Mommy and her bad temper! *That* was good for my ego! All of us worked at it together.

It begins with *me, I* discovered, and I've tried to remember that important lesson ever since.

Children imitate everything. I can't imagine what it must be like for a parent to be going through something as stressful as a divorce and having children watching everything. I would think that the parents would have to be extremely careful about which attitudes and actions they display in front of their kid.s

In Children and Divorce *by Archibald Hart (Word Publishing, 1982) we read about a 12 year-old boy whose parents had divorced. If this boy emulated his mother, I would think he would learn how to imitate hate, dislike, and distrust.*

"We see my dad every second weekend," he said. "When he picks us up (my younger brother and me), the first thing he tells us is, 'Don't say anything to your mother about my new apartment and things: It only upsets her!' As soon as we get home in the evening, Mom asks us lots and lots of questions about where we went and what went on, about his apartment and who was there, and what did they say. I try not to tell her anything, but later she gets me to say something. I say to her, 'Please Mom, don't tell Dad I told you anything!' Five minutes later I hear her shouting at my dad on the telephone about what I said."

We don't want this concept to sound completely negative. There are many positive things that children imitate. The positive attitudes and behaviors should far outweigh the negative. Both my husband and I grew up as pastors' kids. All our lives we have seen examples of service lived out. Service can take many different forms. It may include having an open home so that those in need will be able to take refuge, or it could include traveling to those who need to hear about Jesus.

I am very thankful that both of us had the same sorts of attitudes and behaviors modeled for us. Because of this, when we began our life together, we knew we wanted to model service for those around us. For example, when we lived in Evanston, Illinois, we worked with a local church youth group. One of our greatest joys was being there for the kids whenever they needed us. This didn't mean that they could call us only between 9 A.M. and 9 P.M. It meant receiving knocks on our door and phone calls after many people would have been in bed. These kids needed someone to listen to them at those particular times. The next morning might not have been the right time for them. We thanked the

Lord that during our teenage years we were shown examples of commitment to others in need.

Also, when we had to decide whether or not I should to go to Australia for five weeks, our greatest concern wasn't that Greg would be left on his own, but how I would get time off work. Because we had seen this type of behavior modeled for us all our lives, we realized that temporary separations may be a necessary part of service for some husbands and wives.

Of course it isn't always true that we automatically mirror the emotions or reactions of those around us. We hope to counter the negatives with some positives. Sometimes it is the parent that can turn things around, and at other times it can be the child. Ishmael was able to minister to his mother in the end but not before he underwent some pretty miserable experiences! This is what happened.

Isaac had been born and weaned, and as we have said, the time had come for Sarah and Abraham to celebrate. As custom would have it, a party was in order and the preparations got under way. You can imagine the great joy generated by the occasion. Every child is special, but if you or I had produced our *first* at the grand old age of ninety-one or ninety-nine, we would doubtless have gone to town with the festivities!

What Ishmael didn't realize was that Sarah was watching him watching Isaac. Understandably she didn't appreciate Ishmael's behavior. It didn't take many minutes for her to find her husband and demand that he "get rid of that slave woman and her son, for that slave woman's son will never share in the inheritance with my son Isaac" (Genesis 21:9).

Notice it is fifteen years after the last real family crisis, but poor Hagar is still being called "that slave woman," and Ishmael is now "her [Hagar's] son," though it had been Sarah who had engineered his existence in the first place. It certainly appears to be unfair in the extreme on Sarah's part. Add the fact that there was no place for Abraham to send Hagar and Ishmael, and Abraham knew he had a real family dilemma on his hands!

Abraham's Faith

Since Sarah is rather hard to love at this point, it's good that Abraham shows up in a somewhat better light! The Bible tells us he was greatly distressed about the boy and his maidservant (Genesis 21:12). I'm glad about that. We also read, "The matter distressed Abraham greatly because it concerned his son" (Genesis 21:11). I'm glad about that too! As his holy habit was, Abraham immediately prayed about it, and I'm very glad we have the account of that particular prayer because the patriarch's actions following his prayer time would be somewhat difficult to explain if we were not told specifically that he was obeying God's orders.

God assured Abraham He was going to look after Ishmael and he, Abraham, was to listen to Sarah. Not because she was lovingly directing him to do the will of the Lord, but because she was right in one respect—God had indeed already planned to use Isaac in His purpose of redemption. This, of course, was not news to Abraham, but he was undoubtedly greatly encouraged and was able to trust God for the outcome and not take matters into his own hands again. No doubt the patriarch spent long hours praying about the dark morning ahead, mourning the morrow that had to come and the ensuing separation from Hagar and Ishmael. Abraham, amazing as it may be, was called of God to give up both his sons, not just one of them. Apparently it's an extremely costly business to be a friend of God!

Early the next morning, Abraham took some food and a skin of water and gave them to Hagar. The Bible says he set them on her shoulders and then sent her off with the boy. The text says simply, "She went on her way and wandered in the desert of Beersheba" (Genesis 21:14).

I can't help wondering how Abraham's day continued. Can you imagine how he felt? Perhaps you can't because you are a Hagar. Maybe you too have been sent on your way into a desert of despair by your husband! The supplies he "put on your shoulders" seemed to you (as they must have seemed to Hagar) a total mockery. How would only a skin of water and a little bit of food keep them alive for long?

Rejection

However terrible Hagar's plight, we must not minimize Abraham's agony. Yet perhaps the most desperately unhappy character of all in this dreadful drama was young Ishmael. How was he *feeling*? We have to wonder! Here he was, cast off by his father and his stepmother, alone in a hostile and frightening environment, and his supplies were diminishing rapidly. And why? All because he'd given his little brother a hard time? Imagine the thoughts racing through the youngster's mind. First, thoughts about Abraham. How on earth could his "godly" father do such an "ungodly" thing to them? I doubt if he understood for a minute that his father was greatly distressed about it all. You can almost hear him responding to that thought with a teenager's cynical, "Oh sure!" It would be easier to believe his stepmother had no compunction in sending them to a probable early death. He was well aware he had disappeared from Sarah's thinking the moment she got pregnant with Isaac!

I would imagine Ishmael was kicking himself for his part in this whole mess. Maybe he was thinking that this was such a big punishment for such a little mistake. Perhaps he felt helpless because he knew that being sorry wouldn't change anything. He had only ridiculed his little brother. Did they really deserve such a strong punishment? I think Ishmael's action was only the last straw. However, he probably believed his mocking had caused his current predicament. Many people blame themselves for things that aren't necessarily their fault.

This may happen often with children who are from separated or divorced homes. One church that holds special workshops for people who are separated or divorced finds that the seminar for children, which is always packed to overflowin,g is the one entitled "Is It My Fault."

Ishmael probably wasn't aware of the struggle that Abraham was going through in his own heart. Ishmael was his son too. Abraham knew that he was sending Ishmael away to almost certain death. Yet God had spoken to Abraham and told him everything would be all right. I wonder if Ishmael was aware of this conversation. Maybe Ishmael thought his father had totally rejected him and didn't love him anymore. In a sense, Abraham's actions would verify this interpretation. In this situation all Abraham could do was hold onto the thread of hope that God had given him. God had sai , "I will make the son of the maidservant into a nation also, because he is your offspring" (Genesis 21:13).

Because kids don't know all of the facts behind a given situation, they—like Ishmael— may misinterpret their fathers' or mothers' absences. When I was growing up in England my father used to travel to the United States for months of every year. This meant he really didn't spend much time with our family. Though I was young, I thought I understood why my dad was away so much. However, years later, my parents told me that the night my dad would leave for the States, I would start sleepwalking. I would stop sleepwalking the night he came home. I thought I understood and accepted his absence, but I must have had some problems with it too.

If Ishmael was struggling with the strange, seemingly bizarre actions of Abraham and Sarah, he was soon to face another apparent rejection. The two "refugees" wandered around in the desert of Beersheba until the water in the skin was spent and the food was gone. You can't last in a desert very long after the water has run out, and Ishmael began to dehydrate quickly. Hagar, tough and strong, lasted a little bit longer, and she had just enough strength to support her son for a few more miles before laying him down gently under a scrub bush. Then she went a little way off because she couldn't stand to watch him die. She couldn't bear to see his death throes. Sitting there a little distance away she began to sob uncontrollably (Genesis 21:16). It was at this desperate point God intervened. Hagar and Ishmael were about to find out they were not alone!

Do you think Ishmael understood why Hagar left him to die under the bush? We are not even sure that we know the reasons. As Mom has said, she probably couldn't bear to watch the son she loved so much die. She knew that there was nothing more she could do for Ishmael. She didn't have any hope. Perhaps she was having such a difficult time handling her own grief that she couldn't deal with someone else's problems as well. I feel very sorry for both Hagar and Ishmael. They must have felt so alone; they didn't even have each other's company.

Today, there are many hurting people in the world who must feel as lonely as Hagar and Ishmael. We may feel that our hands are full because we are dealing with our own problems or we may not be able to bear watching someone go through sorrows because we feel helpless. Yet maybe all these people need is for you to reach out to them and show or tell them that you love them.

Years ago, Mom and I were speaking at a mother-daughter weekend. The last session of our seminar was a question-and-answer time. During this session we divided into two groups. Mom answered the mothers' questions, while I tried to answer the daughters' questions. On this particular occasion there were some really tough questions. One was so difficult that I thought my mom should handle it. After the session ended I took the girl back to our cabin to wait for Mom and when she arrived we talked through the situation for over an hour. Finally the young woman thought she felt better. Just as she was about to leave, my mom gave her a hug of encouragement. At this point the tears came. This girl clung to my mom and sobbed and sobbed. I wondered when the last time was that someone had hugged her and told her she was loved.

I heard the story of a desperate young mother who called a female pastor of her church with the news that her husband was about to walk out on her. The wife and mother was hysterical so the pastor jumped in her car and hurried over to the house. When the pastor entered the house the whole place was in disarray. The husband was upstairs packing and the mother was trying to attend to the children. Suddenly, the father appeared and headed toward the door. At this point his small daughter told him to wait. Sobbing, she ran upstairs and smashed open her piggy bank. Then, with the broken pieces of the bank and the money clutched in her tiny hands, she scrambled down the stairs to her father. Throwing the money at him, she begged him to stay, promising to give him all of her money if he would stay with them.

In the aftermath of this heartbreaking scene, the pastor was able to give that devastated young mother a loving touch—she put her arms around her and stayed a long time just holding her. It gave the woman assurance and helped to pull her together. The ministry of *touch* and *presence* is a very real help in times of trouble.

TALK TIME

Share a story about how your family adjusted when someone "new" came to live with you (a baby, grandparent, a stepparent, etc.)

Share some reasons why siblings get jealous.

Discuss the phrase "Children don't create your attitude—they reveal it!"

Share an example if appropriate.

How would you have felt at this point in the story if you were:

Abraham

Sarah

Hagar

Ishmael

THINK TIME

Read Joseph's story in Genesis 37. In groups of two, discuss the following:

Who played favorites?

How did it affect Joseph?

How did it affect Joseph's brothers?

What is the moral of the story?

On your own answer the following questions:

Think about your family relationships. Try to be honest. Do you have a favorite family member? A parent? A child?
Why do you think this is?

Is it causing problems?

Pray about the above situation, if necessary.

PRAYER TIME

1. Spend time thinking about the following.
   Think about changes in your family.
   Think of one "good" thing about the changes; pray about it.
   Think of a negative thing about the changes; pray about it.

2. Pray about the following concerns.
   Pray about sibling rivalry.
   Pray for the "competitors" (the kids).
   Pray for the "referees" (the parents).
   Pray for stepparents and their blended families.
   Pray for stepchildren and their unique positions.

3. Do you see your children modeling themselves after you? Is that good or bad? Pray about it.

ACTION TIME

Purpose:
Motivate church members to actively help the homeless in their community.

Action ideas:
Adopt a homeless family and help them to find housing.

Set up a food pantry or contribute to another church's food pantry.

Work with other churches to provide home-cooked meals for shelters or motels that house the homeless.

Collect clothing for the homeless.

Volunteer to tutor parents and/or children who are homeless.

A plan for adopting a homeless family:
1. Objectives
    Help a specific family find a home.
    Help to personalize the plight of the homeless for your church.

2. Specific procedure
    Speak with the church leadership and determine if this action is appropriate for your church.
    Set up a committee.
    Get as many people in the church involved as possible.
    You should have representatives on the committee for the following subcommittees:
    - Housing
    - Food
    - Clothing
    - Transportation
    - Furniture

    Speak with community social service agencies.
    They will be able to help you find a family.
    There may be an existing program in which you can participate.

    Help to increase the awareness of the church about the homeless situation in general and your "adopted" family in particular.
    Have a regular section in the church bulletin for announcements about your family.
    Have special speakers talk to different groups within the church.

    Once you have a family, deal with their day-to-day needs while you are trying to find a home for them.
    If the family has nowhere to obtain hot food, set up a calendar in the lobby. People should sign up to take them meals.
    If the family has access to cooking facilities, collect canned goods and other items to give to them.
    If the family needs clothing, make an announcement to the church. Provide sizes and locations where the clothes can be deposited.
    If the family needs help with transportation, have someone take charge of finding people to drive the family. Or if there is public transportation, have someone help the family determine which form of transportation will meet their needs.

- Collect furniture and other appliances while you are looking for a home.
- Keep praying and searching. Don't get discouraged. It can be a long process.

CHAPTER SIX
COMMUNION

Principles of Prayer

Prayer is communication with God—the speaking part of our relationship with Him. The principle of prayer would play an important part in Ishmael's survival in the cruel, hard, unresponsive world in which he found himself when his family structure was torn apart. Ishmael fortunately had picked up the huge importance of intercession. I cannot emphasize enough the necessity of prayer. When life deals you its bitterest blows, may you be found praying, and may your children know how to pray too! As Ishmael discovered, it's a good thing to learn these lessons well before Abraham puts a flask of water on your shoulder and sends you off into an uncertain and forebidding future! The entire story teaches us much about the subject of prayer, its principles, and its answers.

In the biblical narrative Abraham is found almost constantly in prayer. God is always talking to him, and he is always talking to God. We can backtrack in our story to find some examples of this constant communication.

Looking at Genesis 12 we see that God spoke to Abram and told him to leave his comfortable home life and wander in the wilderness. Abram trusted God, picked up all his belongings, and went on his way. During his journey, God spoke to Abram, and Abram called on the name of the Lord. Over and over we see that God promised Abram that he would have many descendants and all the land would belong to them. However, at this time, Abram was still childless. He wasn't afraid to tell the Lord that the covenant couldn't be kept through his offspring because he didn't have any children. God reassured Abram that He would take care of everything.

Another time Abraham asked God if Ishmael could be his heir. God had explained He had another child in mind for that privilege, namely Isaac (who had not been born), but He told Abraham to take Ishmael and circumcise him. No doubt Abraham would have shared the great importance of that particular religious rite with Ishmael. I can hear him explaining to his boy, "This means you will be included in the covenant, Ishmael! God is surely smiling on you with favor and planning for you in love." God actually had a specific future of blessing in mind for Ishmael. "I will make him fruitful and will greatly increase his numbers. He will be the father of twelve rulers, and I will make him into a great nation," He said (Genesis 17:20). Even though God knew all things, which included the fact that Ishmael would grow up to be a wild man (Genesis 16:12), God promised the boy He would bless him with twelve sons, and everyone knew the blessing of sons meant God was surely smiling!

Perhaps it was remembering these promises that God had given to Abraham in prayer, and that his father must have shared with him, that turned Ishmael around and helped him to cry out to God when he needed Him. We parents must do our part in teaching prayer, and then we can expect God to do His part.

In Genesis 18 we see that God appears to Abraham again. In person, He confirms that Sarah will have a son. Remember how Sarah laughed at this news? Can you blame her? She and Abraham were quite old. The Lord's answer to Sarah's laughter is very important. He said, "Is anything too hard for the Lord?" (Genesis 18:14) Some may think that after all the times God had stood by Abraham and Sarah, it is a little surprising that they were still doubting the Lord. Yet we do this at times. Though we may claim we are in constant touch with God, sometimes we don't put our faith in Him and believe that He really can make the difference.

During this same visit Abraham pleaded for Sodom. He begged the Lord to save the city that was extremely sinful even if only ten righteous people lived there. Though God destroyed Sodom and Gomorrah, the Bible says He remembered Abraham, and for his sake the angels of the Lord brought Lot and his family out of Sodom before the cities were destroyed.

As we progress through the Book of Genesis, we see many other examples of how God and Abraham were in constant communication. For example, it may surprise you to see that in Genesis 20, once again, Abraham calls Sarah his sister. When Abraham and Sarah were living in Gerar, King Abimelech sent for Sarah so that she could prepare to become his wife. (Doesn't this sound familiar?) However, God appeared to the king in a dream and told him that Sarah was a married woman. In addition God closed all the wombs of all the women living in Abimelech's home. Immediately Abimelech returned Sarah to Abraham. Then Abraham prayed to God to heal the king and his household.

When I read about the relationship between Abraham and God, I am reminded of a couple of principles about prayer. First, I shouldn't be afraid to ask the Lord for help in my times of need. However, I also should remember to communicate with the Lord when everything is running smoothly. I need to become as comfortable talking with God as I am in communicating with my best friends. Think how boring and depressed you would feel if your friends talked with you only when they were in trouble? Wouldn't you miss hearing all about their joys and triumphs? We have to remember that Jesus is our Friend and talk with Him about everything.

I have always been careful to share with my children not only the fact that I am praying for them, but also the answers to my prayers. This I know has had a profound effect on my family. I remember Judy saying anxiously, "I don't want to be in the church youth group, and I *don't* want you praying about it, Mother!" That was a long time ago, but it encouraged me to realize my daughter was learning the power of prayer! This practice of sharing answers has certainly not resulted in our children leaving me to do it, but rather in stimulating a desire to have some answers of their own to share!

That's true. Sometimes we may want to pray for things that we don't deserve. When my younger brother was in fourth grade, he was in the school band. One day as he left for school, he asked Mom to pray for him. He was trying out for first-chair clarinet. My mother looked shocked. She wondered aloud how he could possibly expect her to pray for this request when he hadn't practiced in months. My brother looked innocently at Mom and said that if he had practiced then he wouldn't need to ask her to pray for him!

At other times I have found that people I don't even know have prayed for me during a time of need. I think this is one of the privileges of being a pastor's child. Over the years I have been introduced to people who have prayed daily for me. This has been such an encouragement to me. I really wonder what would have happened in certain situations if these people hadn't been praying diligently.

After my senior year in high school my father took me on a trip. He wanted to show me the types of things he was doing when he was away from our family for months at a time. This was an opportunity for Dad and me to spend some quality time together. Well, our first stop was Bangladesh. We spent the first few days in a large city and then headed into the remote villages to visit some of the missionaries supported by the church. For some reason on the morning we were supposed to return to the city, I began to feel very sick. Within a couple of hours I couldn't lift my head from the pillow. I had a pounding headache and a fever. The missionaries and Dad tried to figure out the best way to get me back to town. Finally, they put a mattress in the back of a van and I stretched out on it for the whole trip. It took me most of the next week to recover from this illness. Later my dad told me he had been very scared. He said that he didn't know what they would have done if the illness had progressed any further because we had been in a remote village. There wasn't a hospital in the area!

My mom didn't know any of this had happened until we arrived home five weeks later. When she heard the story, she just shook her head. She had received a letter from a missionary in Africa, asking if Dad and I were all right. At the time Mom thought we were fine. The missionary explained that on a specific night she had awakened feeling she should pray for us She didn't have any idea as to what if anything was the matter. In fact, she had no way of knowing that Dad and I were away on a trip together. After hearing our story Mom went back to the letter. Sure enough, the dates matched perfectly.

This is a wonderful example of the power of prayer. Sometimes we may not be able to pray for those we love because we don't know that they need specific prayer. Yet God knows all of our needs. He will take care of those we love. He may do this by using other people to pray for our loved ones.

This is a good idea in many ways as we may find ourselves so traumatized by the situation that all we can do is cry! But what happens if, like Hagar, there is no one around to help us pray for our children and we are "out of it"?

Fear or Faith
After Hagar had left Ishmael under a tree so she wouldn't have to watch him die, she sat down a little way off. Both mother and son were crying, alone with their own agonies. But apparently there was a difference! Hagar cried uncontrollably, while Ishmael managed to turn his tearstained face Godward! "God heard the boy crying" (Genesis 21:17). Tears talk, but we also should try to talk to God through our tears. God responded to Ishmael's prayer.

By now Ishmael was far too weak to help himself. His life was nearly spent, but God had heard his prayer and suggested Hagar quit crying and open her eyes to the possibilities around her. She did dry her tears then, and there was a *well* right under her very nose. She had not even seen it because she had been crying so hard.

Isn't that just like us? We get so self-absorbed when we are in the depths of despair that sometimes we miss God's marvelous provision. Prayer is a weapon we seldom use enough in our fight to survive. It is too often replaced by terrible tears of trauma and terror thatdim our sight so we cannot see God's answer to our dilemmas.

This reminds me of Mary Magdalene, crying terrible tears of trouble outside the empty tomb. Faced with the risen Christ, the answer to her woes, she found she couldn't see Him clearly, presumably because she was weeping so hard. "Thinking he was the gardener, she said, 'Sir, if you have carried him away, tell me where you have put him, and I will get him.' Jesus said to her, 'Mary.' She turned toward him and cried out in Aramaic, "Rabboni!" (John 20:15-16).

God often comes to us as He came to Mary and to Hagar, and in the words of the *King James Bible*, asks us, "Woman, why weepest thou? whom seekest thou?" He whom we seek, or the answer to our prayer, is sometimes right there in front of us! We need to stop crying and start functioning again.

And what of the statement of Scripture concerning Ishmael, "God has heard the boy crying as he lies there"? What a promise for youngsters who feel like dying of despair because of their family situations. The teenagers smothering their sobs in their pillows need someone to tell them that God hears their voices just where they are.

I have a friend whose daughter found herself a "crying cupboard." It was a small, isolated place in the attic of her home. She would crawl to it whenever her parents began to fight with each other, and in this place she would be shut up safely with her misery. Her parents, totally self-absorbed with their marriage problems, thought she was doing just fine. They never saw the tears of fear and sorrow she shed as she crouched in the dark. But God saw them. He heard "the voice of the little girl just where she was." He spoke to her mother and brought her to Himself and eventually the father too found the Lord. In the end God brought the whole family to Himself for His work and service.

We must never, never underestimate the power of prayer, the person praying, or how well or badly it is done! It was a child's prayer that touched the heart of God. This story shows us so clearly that He has a special ear for His little ones, and though the scars of Ishmael's terrible experience would probably mark his life forever, he learned that his father Abraham's God was his God too. Answered prayer was all part of that promised covenant that Abraham had told Ishmael about as a young lad.

Family Prayer
So Ishmael had seen prayer modeled in the ordinary course of his daily doings. Abraham acted as priest for his family, and the little boy would breathe the breath of prayer on a regular basis. There is nothing healthier than practicing prayer as a family. One wonders if Hagar and Ishmael prayed together, as we do today, or privately and apart. Whatever the custom of the day, prayer was surely a habit in Abraham's tent.

If such a decision to pray together could be made by your family, then I know only good would come of it. I cannot count the times the Lord has answered the prayers of our own family members. As our children grew older and began to spin off the family "turntable" away from home, the college years gave us lots of opportunities to share individual concerns. The Thanksgiving table became a sacred meeting place for us, and after the food was eaten and news of friends and fun excitedly shared, we would pass the Communion cup and think about Jesus Christ our Savior. Then we would share personal needs around the table and pray for the person on our left. We never shared without laughter, we never shared without tears, and we never shared without commenting with wonder and thankfulness about some request from the last family gathering that had been answered.

What a joy it was for Stuart and me to be gathered in our new son-in-law and daughter's home for our family Thanksgiving shortly after their wedding and to see the Communion cup standing on the table. We shared our tales and tears all over again, as the next generation emulated their parents' tradition and began to care for each other in prayer.

Whatever Ishmael saw of Abraham's prayer life, it was enough to help him in his extremity. Never shortchange the little you think you have done for your children in the way of their religious training if you have been a woman or man of prayer and you have somehow let them know it. Then you have done the very best thing you could possibly have done! I have tried to make it a lifelong habit to do this. I have let my children watch me pray. This was not always easy! It's very difficult to pray when three preschoolers are

climbing all over your life. But watch me, they did! I am reminded of the modeling of such by Mrs. Hudson Taylor for her nine children. Having nine children is enough to

drive any woman into a prayer closet never to come out! However, no such escape was available for the lady, so when she reached her limit, she would throw her apron

over her head and sit like that right in the middle of the chaos her children engendered. They would know exactly what was happening and quiet down. The lesson was not lost on any of them, and they grew up modeling after their mother.

In the past Hagar had already experienced her own incredible answers to prayer. Had she not discovered that the God who ever lives ever sees, and the God who ever sees ever lives to help and heal the sick, lead the lost home, and answer the desperate? Was not Ishmael a daily reminder that God heard all men—even women and slaves? Hagar's personal relationship with God appears to have begun by the well of water in the desert of Shur. I cannot believe she didn't grow in the knowledge of God after that! That is pure speculation, of course, as the Scriptures are silent about Hagar's spiritual health. However, her circumstances for those fifteen hard years with Sarai would certainly force her into a life of trust and fellowship with the Lord. Yet Hagar didn't do very well with prayer at the moment of crisis. She did manage to pull herself together enough to at least become the answer to her child's cry for help. Notice too that Hagar did a very practical thing for her son. In Genesis 21:19 we see that she gave him a drink of water. She didn't preach a sermon exhorting him to trust the Lord or suggest a Bible verse to memorize as he passed into eternity. She demonstrated her trust in the Lord and the truth of the Bible by practically caring for him in his time of need. The answers to our children's prayers often come in the most concrete and practical terms.

Children, especially small ones, cannot think in abstract terms. They reason in the concrete. They ask God for a sunny day, or a pet to keep them company, a new toy for Christmas, or for a visit from Grandpa and Grandma. Perhaps behind all these requests lies the abstract need. The sunny day so they can enjoy playing with little friends who satisfy their needs for meaningful relationships; a pet to keep them company because their fathers are never around to play with them; a new toy for Christmas because they are left on their own too long to entertain themselves; and a visit from grandparents to supply a security need in their little lives. Whatever they ask for according to their felt needs, God seeks to answer according to their real needs. Ishmael needed water, but Ishmael's need for water went far beyond his body's desperate need for moisture. He needed water in order to live and grow up and have a family, to experience the good things God provides for those who love Him. God first answered his felt need in a practical way, so He could answer his real needs later on.

If we want to *be* the answer to someone else's prayers, we need to stop crying long enough to look around for the well of water so we can save the situation! In Hagar's case, she was the only one who could become a living, loving answer to Ishmael's prayer, and that realization must have provided the impetus to do *something*. The problem with our desperate situations is that too often we do not count ourselves *that* important to the someone who is in need. But I would suggest that you would do well to just presume it! Presume "Ishmael," whoever he is, is totally dependent on you. This way, you will drag yourself out of your own troubles to attend to his! Unless you start to believe Ishmael has no way of surviving unless you get involved, you probably won't! It must have been tempting for Hagar to hope a passing stranger would hear her boy—a warmhearted shepherd perhaps, or another mother on her way to the well. Maybe a strong person would happen along with plenty of resources. But no, God called Hagar to become the answer to her own child's prayers, and what is more, He showed her how to do it. After all, no one loved Ishmael like Hagar! Why should anyone care as much as she? Why should anyone else put himself out to find practical ways of solving their problem?

Why do we leave the pastor, youth leader, Sunday School teacher, or counselor to answer the prayers and practical needs of our children? As mothers, it's our responsibility to pray and our responsibility to become the answer, and often that means *doing* something concrete to relieve the situation.

Doing It Themselves

It's very important that children not only see adults modeling prayer, but are encouraged to talk to God themselves from as early an age as possible. Children find little or no difficulty with this if they are encouraged from an early age. One of our grandsons is growing up fast. Every month I drive to his home and get my "Grandma injection"! What joy to play and read and take him for walks or to the park to see the animals in the small zoo. Coming up to three years of age, he is finding language a weapon in his fight for early independence! His favorite phrase seems to be, "I do it meself!" This phrase is used from the moment he gets up and begins to peel off his nightwear to the last minute before he drops off to sleep.

"Shall I pray to Jesus?" I asked him brightly last time I parked him in bed with teddy and a menagerie of woolly animals.

"No!" he answered politely but very definitely. "I do it meself!"

I was delighted. His vocabulary is meager to say the least, but he allowed me the privilege of staying to listen as he did it " 'imself," and it was *wonderful*. I thought so, he thought so, and God thought so! I know He did. Children learn by doing and so do adults.

Sometimes it's too easy to allow bedtime prayers to degenerate into "bad time" prayers. So often bedtime can be such a zoo, and it's hard to interject a spiritual sense into it! You may try praying with children at different times of the day: when you cuddle a little one on your knees in front of a warm fire, or after lunch as you rock him or her to sleep. Otherwise, they will be tempted to think that God belongs in the bedroom, is locked into talking to you at 7 p.m. exactly, and is always a bit of a nuisance when a nice warm mattress waits for their tired little flames.

So try to get the child to pray on his own instead of putting your words into his mouth. As we have seen, Ishmael knew very well how to talk to God. It is much more meaningful for a child to formulate his or her own conversation with the Lord than for you to do it for him or her. Encourage a child to listen as well. From early days, you can develop a little one's expectations of God through the activity of prayer.

As a young mother I would read a story from a children's Bible to our kids and apply *one* truth from it. I would try to help them understand what God was "saying" to them. For example, the story of the Good Samaritan kept them spellbound. One of the lessons of the parable was to teach people who believed in God to be kind to people who hurt. This way they would show by their kindness they belonged to God's family. "God was 'talking' to us through this story," I explained to the children. "Now let's talk back to Him about it," I would suggest. We would then discuss it for a few moments, and I would try to find an application on their own level. For instance, Margaret, a friend of our daughter Judy, had fallen down in the school playground, bruising her knee. I suggested that God wanted Judy to get off the swing (her donkey), and help Margaret to get to the nurse's office (the inn). I said she could even spend her candy money on a chocolate bar to give to Margaret to stop her from crying (a parallel to paying the bill at the inn). Having talked about it, we all prayed about Margaret's knee together. A child can be taught to "listen" to God's Word and "reply" in prayer when he or she is still very young.

Another thing that helps children learn to pray is their enjoyment of fantasy. The fact that children cannot see the people they are talking to is not a problem at all for children. This may be a problem for adults, but children live in a wonderful fantasyland where they talk to dolls that come alive, animals with human voices that talk back to them, and even inanimate objects that turn into talking balls, trees, or houses! How many little children invent an unseen companion? Little ones need to be told of the kind Being who loves them—a gentle, yet strong Heavenly Father who is good and true and who will always listen to them. You'll see; they will use their God-given gift of fantasy to "see" Him and accept Him as their friend with total faith.

So children should certainly learn the importance of prayer by being

COMMUNION

helped by a parent to see prayer modeled and to exercise prayer for themselves. But they should also be the objects of our prayers. The day Abraham sent Hagar and Ishmael away from his tent, I am sure he spent many hours praying for them. I am also certain it would not have been the first time he prayed for them. Good fathers pray for their children! As friction developed between the different members of Abraham's family, I'm sure the patriarch redoubled his efforts in prayer on their behalf. I can see him praying for harmony between Sarah and Hagar, and between Isaac and Ishmael. I believe Abraham prayed such prayers because so many times we read about the prayers he prayed for other people. His prayers didn't always get answered, and neither will ours, but imagine what chaos there would have been if he hadn't prayed at all!

You might be tempted to wonder if God does indeed answer prayer. After all, the conflict was not resolved with Hagar and the child, despite prayer. But don't forget the fifteen years of everyday living between the clashes! Believing as I do in the restraining power of prayer, it is no surprise at all to learn that Hagar and Ishmael lived with Sarah and Isaac for a considerable period before real trouble erupted again.

The problem with practicing prayer is the problem of finding and making time for it. If you think you struggle with this, think about Hagar! As a young mother with huge problems, she must have known the necessity of prayer very well. But because she was a slave, she would have little, if any, free time to exercise it! We, however, are not slaves.

2. The present state of your prayer life.

We are free. However busy a young mother is, she is busy doing what *she* decides she wants to do. It's a question of making a choice that whatever else you do for your children, you will pray for them, regularly and diligently. Praying mothers give their children the rarest gift in the world.

When our little ones ran around the lovely English Lake District, their steps were bathed in prayer. When their teenage strides took them into the American school system, they were dressed by prayer for the battle. And when as young adults they found themselves thinking through their faith, prayer clothed their minds with arguments that won the day. They would call home at all times of the day and night when particular stresses would occur, making sure we were praying for them. That knowledge, they told us later, reassured, comforted, and fortified their own convictions and strengthened their own prayer lives. Prayer should never be the last resort, but the very first thought of the day.

Remember, no matter is too small to pray about. You don't learn to pray with your last breath! A very close friend used to tell me she didn't feel the Almighty should be bothered with tiny trivialities, only with big things. But how can we doubt His interest when we see His creation and find a tiny, exquisite flower no bigger than a fingernail that grows on a mountain so big it fills the skyline? Can we doubt His interest in our little woes when we count a baby's tiny toes and observe how God made his silky eyelashes, even while He spins the earth in space and juggles galaxies? He knows the sparrow falls as surely as He knows the earthquake's force. If you want a good example of this very thing, look at Abraham, and think about the things he talked to God about!

COMMUNION

🌀 TALK TIME

1. Discuss freely:
   The past state of your prayer life.
   The present state of your prayer life.
   What you would like the future state of your prayer life to be.

2. Write a sentence summary answering each of the following questions:
   What needs to be changed to generate a healthier personal prayer life?
   What steps will you take starting this week toward that end?

   Step 1:

   Step 2:

3. Promise God (in prayer) you will follow through.

💡 THINK TIME

Use silent prayer or meditation to focus your thoughts on God—His creation.

Then let your mind contemplate His redemption. (Think about the Cross.)

Continue your "thought journey" to the Resurrection. (Think about the empty tomb.)

Remember the Ascension and the giving of the Holy Spirit at Pentecost.

Praise Him for all these things.

PRAYER TIME

1. As a group praise God for:
   Possibility of prayer.
   Privilege of prayer.
   Answers to prayer.
   Times He has said "No" or "Wait" to your prayers.

2. As a group pray for:
   More personal discipline in prayer.
   More people to be won to Christ through prayer.
   More children to be taught to pray effectively.
   Discouraged "pray-ers" to be encouraged.
   More *church* group prayer.
   More enjoyment of prayer.

ACTION TIME

Purpose:
How to have a regular prayer time with your teenager.

Talk together about having a regular prayer time. Agree to try it for a trial period.

Make the rules together so the child feels part of it. For example, decide:

Duration (10 minutes is adequate)
    Place
    Day of the week
    Time

Share participation. One day you lead; next time let the teenager do it.

Follow this suggested format for five days.
Day One

COMMUNION

—Read a short psalm or ten verses of Scripture.
—Each pick a favorite verse from the reading.
—Each thank God in prayer for the psalm or Scripture and his or her particular verse.
—Make a list of three people you'd each like to pray for. Be sure to share why they need prayer.
—Swap lists and pray.
—Keep prayers short. Finish on time!

Day Two
—Read another psalm or part of one of Paul's letters. Let the leader choose the passage.
—Share a verse you "didn't" like and explain why!
—Together make a list of three family needs.
—Let the teenager pray for them.
—Adult can finish by thanking God that He has heard the requests.

Day Three
—Read alternate verses of the Ten Commandments from Exodus 20.
—Each think of one person who is breaking one of these commandments.
—Both pray for these people. Don't use names.
—Each pick one commandment he or she finds hard to keep.
—Pray for yourselves so that each may keep God's commandments too.

Day Four
—Each read a few verses of Revelation 1.
—Spend time commenting on the different aspects of the vision that John had.
—Talk to God about it. (Equal time—let teen start.)
—Pray for people you both know who don't believe that Christ is truly God.

Day Five
—Read Acts 1:8.
—Make a list of missionaries you know. If you don't know any, make a list of ministers and leaders of the church, youth group, etc.
—Let teenager pray these people will be:

—Encouraged in their work.
—Good witnesses for Christ.
—Let adult pray for the places that need a witness, for example:

   Judea, a local town.
   Samaria, a country.
   Uttermost parts of the earth.

CHAPTER SEVEN
CARING

Responsibility
Children have to learn responsibility. That means someone has to teach them! The Scriptures have something to say to parents in this regard. "Train a child in the way he should go, and when he is old he will not turn from it" (Proverbs 22:6). These words apply not only to the moral realm, but also encourage us to figure out how our children "should go." Another translation renders those particular words *should go* as *according to his bent*. To put it another way, we are to bring up our children the way God meant them to go and not the way we decide they should go! He has gifted them individually and uniquely, and His plan is to give them into the care of loving, responsible parents who will so thoroughly understand their children they will help them discover their bent or gifts. This is not easy as parents often have hidden agendas for their kids, or the children perceive Mom and Dad want them to follow in their footsteps.

This whole idea of parents trying to decide on their children's futures is a scary thought in our society. Some parents try to get their children into the "proper" nursery
schools so that these children will have a chance of going to the "right" grade schools. In this way, the children might be accepted into the "correct" junior high schools, senior high schools and even colleges. It's not that parents shouldn't try to provide the best for their children; however, sometimes it appears (especially when the children are older) that the parents might be doing all this to fulfill their own goals instead of letting their children make their own decisions.
Recently a teenager committed suicide and left a note for his mother

that said he had tried to live up to all her expectations. Yet it didn't seem to matter how "good" he was because it was never enough, therefore he decided to take his own life. This is a sad commentary on our society.

When I entered college, I really thought that God wanted me to go into medicine; however, I wasn't exactly sure. I took quite a few premed courses, but wasn't very settled. In addition, I took a course in psychology and found it very interesting. After finishing my sophomore year I didn't know what to do. I was torn between medicine and psychology. My parents were concerned about my trying to discover my "bent" so they tried to help me obtain as much information as possible so I could make a decision. They listened to me for many hours and tried to help me figure out the pros and cons of both areas of study. They put me in touch with a good friend, a surgeon, who let me follow him around one summer and get a taste of a physician's lifestyle. Obviously, we all prayed about it too. After all this help, I had to make the decision on my own. It wasn't as scary as I thought it would be; in fact, it became very clear that I wanted to go into psychology. I'm sure it wouldn't have been such an easy decision without my parents' information and support.

God's idea was that Hagar should bring up Ishmael to be able to use his talents to look after himself and willingly and gladly care for his parents if the need arose. After Hagar

revived Ishmael, the two began a new life together in the desert.

Like Ishmael, children of single-parent families often find that their changed circumstances thrust new and necessary responsibilities on them. A boy may feel he is now the "man" of the house and must bear that burden bravely. This can be overwhelming to the child, or it can be an incentive to develop in ways that nobody would ever have dreamed possible.

Children whose parents are working may need to take on more responsibility. I think of our own children, particularly David. There were long periods of our son's childhood

when his father was away on business. My struggle was to know how much "extra" a little eight-year-old should be doing around the house. *What was the balance?* I worried.

Would the child begin to resent his father's absence if I asked him to do too much? Fearing this, I would try to make his load lighter than it would have been if his father *had* been around! That wasn't any good at all. I came to realize that David *liked* to feel he was being a real help by getting the coal in for the fire, carrying the shopping in from the car, and caring for the dog. It was through these very experiences that he discovered he could do all sorts of useful things with his hands. He developed certain skills to a high degree of efficiency in those years, skills he has used as he has gone on to maturity.

On the one hand, children learn responsibility by doing things, and on the other hand they learn to do things by being asked to be responsible for them. We parents, however, need to give children the chance to learn these lessons. "Let my kid show me he's a responsible kid, and I'll give him all the responsibility he can handle," a father once said to me.

"Why don't you give him some responsibility when he *isn't* responsible and see what it does for him?" I suggested. Some parents are still waiting for some satisfactory sign or behavior pattern to appear before they will trust their children with a responsible task, a decision to make, or a sibling to watch. I found out our children thrived on challenges!

After our family moved to the United States, my ministry developed. Usually I would travel on the weekends when Stuart was at home; in this way one of us could be with the children. However, one weekend we were going away together. The kids were in their early teens at the time. A very nice young couple agreed to baby-sit, but it did not go well. We couldn't understand why until the kids told us they wanted to be trusted to stay home on their own. The next time both of us were away at the same time, we took a deep breath and tried it. It worked like a dream. When you hear your children asking you to trust them to be responsible, take the risk and go for it. In our case it worked and worked well.

However, we aren't saying that every child is ready for a lot of responsibility. Each parent will probably know how much his or her child can handle. Some children may be too immature, may have been irresponsible in the past, or may lack some necessary experience in order to be trusted. For example, it might not be appropriate to have children take responsibility for a major decision in their lives when they haven't made minor decisions.

Let's return to the story.

Ishmael became an archer, and we presume from this little comment in Genesis 21:20 that he became a very good one! He must have been good enough to provide food for his mother and himself so they could survive. Yet he was only a teenager when he found himself with new and awesome responsibilities. We don't know how much responsibility he had been given by Sarah in the past, but he surely had a double dose thrust on him by Hagar before he had a chance to prove himself to her. However, he appears to have done just fine.

The reason for this may have been Hagar's encouragement. I can't imagine Hagar putting Ishmael down as she watched his arrows falling short of their target as he learned the skills of archery. Rather, I can hear her shouting words of encouragement as she watched from the door of their makeshift shelter. Ishmael would need lots of help from his mother as he grew up in that inhospitable environment.

The Bible talks about *households* rather than families in Ishmael's day. The household would normally embrace the extended family. This would include servants, slaves, and aliens—a huge circle of people in any given household who could give input to the children. Now Ishmael found himself bereft of this wide family circle and alone with his mother.

This can be paralleled to today. Many children, having experienced a loving family corresponding to the biblical household, find themselves suddenly and unexpectedly removed from it all, out of the nest along with a rejected or hurt parent. The sudden necessary responsibilities can be totally overwhelming. Encouragement may be a helpful factor in the response of the child to the situation.

It's hard for the parents, however, to encourage the child when no one is encouraging them! Hagar must have felt so unbelievably alone and isolated. It is at times like these I like to think of Jehovah encouraging Hagar in her heart so that she in turn could put "heart" into her boy. Paul said, "Praise be to the God and Father of our Lord Jesus Christ, the Father of compassion and the God of all comfort, who comforts us in all our troubles, so that we can comfort those in any trouble with the comfort we ourselves have received from God" (2 Corinthians1:3-4). Hagar, we know, had met the One who had seen her plight and had encouraged her once before.

Do you know how to give encouragement to another person? It's simple really, and in our day and age we have a lot more helps around us. A kind word will do it or a few words of written affirmation. You could make a phone call perhaps. If you're English, you can offer an invitation to talk about things over a cup of tea!

One thing is certain—children thrive on encouragement. With words of incentive and praise from his mother, we assume young Ishmael proved the point. He took heart and became an archer!

Encouragement in Times of Need
You know, Mom, I think you and Hagar are alike in some ways. When I first started speaking you were such an encouragement to me. Most of my arrows fell a long way from the target and yet you still encouraged me. First, you would try to find something positive that I did and share that information with me. You would also point out what I did wrong—not in a critical manner but in a way that showed me you loved me, cared for me, and were genuinely interested in helping me become all God wanted me to be. I had a bad habit of saying "um" all the time and I'm still working on speaking slowly. You have to remind me about that a lot.

I can think of lots of other examples of when different members of our family encouraged me. As a sophomore in high school I went out for the cross-country team. At that time David was a senior running on the varsity team. The first day of practice all the girls and guys had to do laps around a park. Obviously, because most of the guys ran faster than most of the girls, David lapped me. As he went past, he put his arm around my shoulder and told me to keep going. Though I quit the team that year, at that point in time he really encouraged me.

Sometimes I think our family has kept the postal service and the telephone company in business. I always know that Mom and Dad are there for me if I need their help. When I was struggling through physics in college, I called home after every exam. In the end, Dad wrote down the dates of my physics exams on his calendar. The phone barely rang once before he would answer and listen to my complaints. Mom, you have sent me so many special handwritten notes over the years. Sometimes they were pages long and other times they were just a few words. Whatever the length, you would always tell me that you loved me and were praying for me. Knowing and being reminded of these things has always been an encouragement to me.

Greg has encouraged me in other ways. One example of his "silent" encouragement was during the summer I was trying to finish my master's thesis. I was working part-time and Greg was working full-time. I would come home from work and write until 1 or 2 in the morning. When Greg came home from work, he would help by reading what I had written and giving me suggestions. One Saturday I looked up from my papers and realized that I hadn't gone grocery shopping, done the laundry, or cleaned the apartment in over a month. Yet all three of these things had been done for me. Greg had done them without even saying a word. He couldn't have picked a better way to help and encourage me at that time in my life.

Here are some practical thoughts concerning parental responsibility and encouragement. First, don't be afraid to challenge teens with responsibility. They may moan and groan about it, but they will end up actually being grateful for the skills they've learned. As a good friend of mine commented about her daughter's sulky face when asked to help with the family dinner, "She's enjoying herself really. She just doesn't know it yet!"

Second, work alongside your children cheerfully! Be positive and as creative as you can to make the task *fun*. If it's a total bore to you, you can be sure it will be a total bore to them! Making a game out of a task or involving children in jobs at a fun level helps take the *mundanity* out of the mundane!

For example, baking can be a bane—especially if you don't like to cook. But baking English shortbread can be transformed for children if you let them score it and draw pictures in the dough while they are doing it!

When I was very young I lived in a small English cottage. This cottage was chilly and drafty in winter, and a roaring fire was important to all of us. One day Mom and Dad discovered the chimney wasn't working properly, so Dad decided to clean it. Unfortunately, the brush got stuck in the chimney. Dad threw a brick down the chimney to dislodge the brush; the brick got stuck too! With these items lodged in the chimney, it was not surprising that it took a long time to light the fire and keep it going!

When Dad was traveling, one of Mom's tasks was to collect sticks for this fire. She decided she could involve David, who was a toddler at the time, in this task. This may sound simple, but remember that this fire was very important to us, and it took a lot of sticks to keep the fire burning. Mom *tried to make this task interesting and fun for David by painting cardboard boxes different colors and having David put the big sticks he collected in the red box, medium-size sticks in the blue box, and small sticks in the yellow box.*

Third, show the child how the task must be done. Be specific. It's not fair to expect a child to *know* without being told! Now I'm sure Hagar wasn't terribly good with a bow and arrow—or maybe she was! Who knows what skills she had picked up? Even if she couldn't help Ishmael too much with his archery, she undoubtedly taught him how to prepare the game once it was shot! It would take both of them to skin and clean the beasts, collect the wood for the fire, and make a spit for the meat. A good mother spells the steps out for the children. I remember getting very upset with one of my children for not setting the table the way I wanted it set. "You never told me how," the child quite rightly objected, "so don't yell at me!" I found I needed to spell it out step-by-step.

Make sure the children know they are accountable to you for the duty that is required of them. The word "responsibility" comes from the Latin word *responsibilities,* which means to require an answer. It helps to know we have to answer to people for our duties and tasks.

Deadlines
It really helps me to have to answer to people for what I am doing. "Answering" can take the form of meeting specific deadlines. I am the type of person who tends to procrastinate unless I know that something is due on a specific date, and there is no way of missing the deadline. Sometimes, if other people don't give me deadlines then I have to make up my own. Otherwise, the work may never get finished. It is not that I don't want to do something or don't find something interesting and exciting. Usually, it just comes down to the fact that I have a lot of things that need to be done at the same time. Deadlines help to prioritize what will get finished and when. We all can relate to deadlines if we think about April 15. How many of us would complete our tax forms if this deadline did not exist?

Finally, don't forget to praise children when they have tried their best. Verbal affirmation can help children to be sure of themselves and their skills. Responsibility gives children a chance to do a job and receive affirmation in the form of praise for it. It also gives an opportunity for correction if the job isn't done satisfactorily, and after all, children who are never corrected feel their actions have no consequences. Therefore, they are of no consequence. If what they *do* matters, then who they *are* matters! Perhaps Hagar, facing the probability of bringing up her teenager all by herself, encouraged herself in the belief that more responsibility can often grow more-responsible people.

One of the best things about responsibility and accountability is the follow-through that they require. Hagar and Ishmael had to eat every day! It was Ishmael's responsibility to develop this skill of archery engendered by their circumstances. He was accountable to his mother to practice it and become proficient at it. Necessity is a great teacher. I can't imagine how Hagar and Ishmael would have fared if Hagar had said to Ishmael, "Why don't you try your hand with a bow and arrow? See if you like it. If you do, that's great. If you don't like it, you can drop it!" They would have starved to death!

I know the responsibilities placed on our children are not nearly so urgent or necessary as Ishmael's archery, but I wonder what message many modern parents give when their children don't follow through with their lesser tasks when they never finish a job. If we go soft on our kids in this regard, we run the danger of being less than all we should be as parents.

TALK TIME

1. Discuss the following quotations.

"Train a child in the way he should go, and when he is old he will not turn from it" (Proverbs 22:6).

"Recently a teenager committed suicide, and left a note for his mother that said that he had tried to live up to all of her expectations. Yet, it didn't seem to matter how "good" he was because it was never enough, therefore he decided to take his own life".

"On the one hand, children learn responsibility by doing things, and on the other hand they learn to do things by being asked to be responsible for them".

2. Work through the following exercises.

   Write one thing someone has done or said to encourage you lately.
   Write one thing you have done or said to encourage someone else.
     Share and discuss.
   Think of one person in your life who needs to be encouraged.
   What will you do for him or her?
   When will you do it?

THINK TIME

Read the verses that follow. Ask yourself: Who was doing the encouraging and who was being encouraged? Why did they need encouragement? What did you learn from this?

   Deuteronomy 1:38
   Acts 20:1-2
   Colossians 2:1-3 (Clue: Read about Laodicea in Revelation 3:14-22.)

PRAYER TIME

1. Praise God for people in your life who have:
   Cared for you
   Trusted you with responsibility
   Encouraged you

2. Pray for parents and children who are in need of care, trust, and encouragement.

3. Some people have no one to pray for them. We can then be an encouragement through prayer. Choose a promise of Scripture and pray it for someone you know.

4. Sit quietly and ask the Holy Spirit to bring someone to mind whose need you could meet. Ask Him how you can meet that need. (You may not want to exert the effort to meet that need, or you may feel inadequate.) Write down a promise to God concerning the action you will take.

ACTION TIME

Purpose:
Starting a "Widow's Might" group for those who walk alone.

1. Identify widows:
   in your congregation
   in your neighborhood
   in your clubs
   Advertise in church bulletin, community paper, supermarkets, etc.

2. Draft a letter of inquiry to those who have identified themselves, asking if they would be interested in a support group.

3. Ask for information.
   Which day of the week would be best for you?
   At what time of day would you like to meet?
   Where would you like to meet?
      church
      home
   Do you need transportation?
   What is your basic need?
   What topics would you like to see covered in such a group?

4. Be certain about your purpose. Brainstorm ideas with a friend and set a tentative agenda for the first meeting. Brainstorm again with the group at the first meeting and prioritize five or six ideas to serve as the main goals of your group. Such a list might include providing time for:
   Bible study
   Prayer

Sharing and caring
Helping others
Practical tips
Social events

5. Plan a "mid-course correction" meeting. For example, after meeting weekly for a few months the ladies in our group decided that they would meet every other week because this would suit their needs better.

6. Help the group to reach out to other lonely folks, and remember—a satisfied customer is the best salesperson for your ministry!

DESERT OF HARDSHIP, WATER OF HOPE

CHAPTER EIGHT
COMMITMENT

Making the Choice

We talk a lot about commitment. We say relationships cannot work without it, and up to a point that is true. But it takes two to make commitment work. One person may commit while the other dallies around, not knowing if he or she wants to own the duty of responding and offering commitment in return. Yet renewed commitment on behalf of one partner or parent can spawn renewed love in a relationship that has grown cold or become careless with age.

Hagar's commitment to Sarah and Abraham was over. Now she had only one other human left in her life with whom to have a commitment: Ishmael. Abruptly, she was

faced with a choice. Realizing the last chapter of her life was over, she knew she could commit herself to her son or could simply sit in her desert of despair, mourn what might

have been, and finish the story right there. "If only I had worked a little harder," she must have been tempted to say. Or, "If only I hadn't despised my mistress so much, then we

might not have had to learn how to do something as mundane as hunt our own food!" We will never build out of the rubble of our broken relationships if we spend our days obsessed with what might have been or what difference we could have made.

When you speak of the way Hagar could have been, it reminds me of myself. I am forever saying that I "should have" done something or said something differently. For

example, remember what I was like after I would finish taking an exam? Instead of forgetting about the test since there was nothing I could do about it anyway, I would

think about what I should have written to specific essay questions or contemplate what I would have written if I had had more time. Looking back I realize how futile this

approach really was. I ended up exhausted from worrying and thinking about something that could not be changed. Instead, I should have shrugged my shoulders, waited for

the results, and then if necessary, figured out ways I could avoid the same mistakes next time.

I know this next example will sound strange to some people, yet I bet if you think about it, you will realize that it isn't so weird. On separate occasions, both my mother

and my husband have told me that they can't stand to go shoe shopping with me. In fact, both have refused to go shoe shopping with me. At first I thought they were the

ones who were strange. However, hearing the same thing from two people on two separate occasions made me wonder, and I concluded that they were probably right.

First, I have a very difficult time even finding a pair of shoes that I like. I'm told I circle a store in about two seconds flat. I explained to Mom and Greg that I know exactly what I want so if I don't see anything I like then why should I waste my time in the store? They both pointed out to me that this isn't quite true because even when I find what I want and buy it, the whole ride home I wonder aloud if I should have spent the money on the shoes, if the shoes will really match the outfits that I bought them for, and if I really like them after all.

I also tend to second-guess conversations. Sometimes, when Greg and I return from dinner with friends, I will sit and worry about something I said during the meal I will say to Greg, "I should have been more understanding" or, "Why didn't I say this instead of that?" Now there is nothing wrong with wondering these things, but I tend to go overboard mulling over the same scene in my mind. This doesn't help anything. Nothing that has happened can be changed. In fact, by doing this I may be preventing myself from moving forward in relationships. Instead I should be thinking about what I can do in the future to rectify the situation or make sure that I don't make the same mistakes in other relationships.

COMMITMENT

Obviously Hagar didn't spend the rest of her life immobilized by second-guessing her circumstances.

The best thing to do in a Hagar dilemma is to look around to find at least *one* person who might need you to commit yourself to him or her—and do it! Decide that, whatever their response, you'll do *your* part with every last ounce of strength you have. When Hagar dragged herself up from the sand in order to bring Ishmael water, she began a whole new phase of her life. Ishmael needed her. She would begin there!

I believe you will always be able to find someone who needs you. This old hurting world is too full of needy people to ever run out of "Ishmaels." Yet though we might have a desperate Ishmael right under our noses, we may find ourselves so immobilized by the past that we leave him there to die. One reason we may be so willfully still is the forgiveness factor. If we have not forgiven, we cannot seem to give again to anybody! Harboring grudges doesn't release creative energy, but rather burns us up with bitterness, fueling our hurt and self-pity until we are destroyed ourselves.

I remember my mother-in-law feeling bereft and devastated by the sudden death of her husband. He had gone to heaven in a moment, in the twinkling of an eye! The heart attack had come suddenly and terribly without warning. We had been married a few years, and Bernard, Stuart's brother, was in the navy. Now Mother had no one to lavish her love and attention on. Her whole life had been totally devoted to caring for and serving her family, and now her husband and sons were gone. She began to react bitterly, saying to my husband, "You've all left me; now what do I do?" Stuart gently pointed out that Pop hadn't left by choice, and Bernard had been called up by the navy. Though they had all left, life must go on. He suggested we all pray about finding an "Ishmael" who needed her. With characteristic character, grit, and determination, Mother soon accepted the challenge, and before we knew what was happening, she had invited a young man needing a home and some practical needs to be met to come and live in the large family house with her. He came with alacrity, and both Mother and the young man benefited hugely from the arrangement. The empty nest need never be empty when the world is so full of birds without nests of their own or with broken wings!

Talk about birds with broken wings! Just look at Ishmael now. Add Hagar's total despair and the desperate physical danger for both in the desert heat and you wonder how they could possibly survive—never mind start again! Yet somewhere deep down within the human heart there lies an insatiable will to live. I have seen people in the most ferocious human dilemmas hope where there is no hope, try when it appears totally futile to try, and decide they are going to summon every single outer and inner resource known to man and commit to life! Have you committed yourself to life? Or are you waiting until death ends it all and the chance for new commitment is over?

Hagar knew all about commitment. Hadn't she committed herself to serving Abraham's family all these years? But now she was looking at the broken pieces of her commitment that had been flung in her face, and she knew the time had come to leave them buried in the sand and turn her full attention to the here and now—and to Ishmael.

My mother-in-law had to forgive Pop for going to heaven, Stuart for marrying me, and Bernard for serving in the Royal Navy. That's an awful lot of forgiving to do! However, it might not sound hard at all to someone who has to forgive a husband for rejecting her or a parent for abuse. If bitterness is eating your heart out and "what-might-have-been" inertia is preventing your recovery, it doesn't much matter how big the reason for the bitterness! It's hard to think about commitment *again* when all your time and best efforts have either come to naught, failed, or are no longer needed. We may think that if what seems to be a lifetime of love and service has come to an end with no positive results, what's to stop the next situation from ending up exactly the same way? And yet many people who encounter these situations do not give up.

Once Greg and I were asked to house-sit while a couple was away on vacation. The couple also had teenagers in high school whom we were supposed to supervise. We had worked with the teens in a youth group, the family had a beautiful home, and they were actually going to pay us to live there for a week. I thought we were in for a fun, easy week. I was wrong. Those two teenagers were a real handful—smoking in the bedroom, getting drunk, and denting their parents' car. Dealing with all this didn't leave much breathing time!

You could have said, "Well, those kids behaved so badly, and flung our commitment in our face, so why try to help anyone else again? Let the ministry die and get out of youth work."

COMMITMENT

I guess we could have said this, but we didn't. We knew that these kids had specific problems that we might be able to help them with. We told them that we were very disappointed in them. Yet we also told them that the week hadn't changed our minds about them. We still loved them and wanted them to be involved in the youth ministry.

Something similar to this experience can happen in any relationship. Just think how many more divorces there would be if, every time a person did something that upset his or her partner, the partner decided to give up on the commitment to the relationship. We all have to learn to forgive and move forward in our relationships.

So we must work hard to prevent the past from paralyzing the present and determining the future. New commitments need to come after you see you have done all you can with the past and after past abuses have been forgiven. Then we will be free to attend to building up relationships that need and merit *all* our attention!

You may wonder what happens if you cannot forgive and forget. Perhaps we could suggest it's a question of *will not* rather than *cannot*. Forgiveness is a command and, therefore, not to be confused with feelings. It involves the will. We are to forgive our friends, relatives, and enemies because Jesus said we must. We are to pray for those who spitefully use us. What is more, we are to forgive them as freely as God has forgiven us! We can begin that process by being obedient and saying the words, "I forgive them," in prayer. If possible and appropriate, face them and tell them as well as God! Don't worry about the feelings you have about it all. Your feelings may take years to catch up with your words because your feelings have probably been on the rack. But let your words begin to say what you know is the *right* thing to say. *Doing* the right thing is far more important than *feeling* the right thing!

I think the thing that helps me to forgive people is the knowledge that it's something God has told me to do. It's right. I'm an old enough Christian to know I don't always *feel* like doing what is right.

The danger with harboring an unforgiving spirit is the blackout it produces in your mind's eye. Jesus said our eye must be clear (Matthew 6:22). We must have a single-minded insistence on letting God's light reveal anything *dark* in our lives—such as a bitter spirit (Psalm 139:23). Having revealed the darkness to us, it behooves us to deal with it. So often we choose to leave the darkness there and get on with the rest of life as we "see" it. It's as if we can get our own back by refusing to forgive. The problem is that our lives then become like the lighthouse whose window on one side was blown out by a storm. The lighthouse keeper didn't see any harm in boarding up the hole and putting off replacing the window for a few weeks. After all, the light was shining brightly from all the other sides of the lighthouse. Shortly afterward, during another storm, a boat foundered on the rocks. It had approached the shore on the dark side of the lighthouse! An Ishmael might founder on the rocks of life if we choose to leave one dark part in our lives. Only God can help us "see" clearly again. He wants to replace the black despair with transparent glass!

The next thing to remember is to leave the judging up to Him. If the people who have wronged me deserve the Father's frown, or worse—be assured the Father will frown, or worse! We are told that wrongs will be righted and rights will be rewarded one day. Not this day perhaps, or even one day soon, but one final day it will be seen to, and we mustn't try to fiddle with the hands on God's clock! We can neither put God's clock forward *nor* back, for we have been given only today. Today is where we are and where Ishmael needs us! Let us forgive Abraham and Sarah and attend to his needs.

Both Hagar and Ishmael had to commit themselves to each other. Hagar and Ishmael showed their commitment to making their relationship work by responding to each other and lowering or changing their expectations For example, Ishmael accepted the wife that his mother picked for him. In Genesis 21:21 we see that while Hagar and Ishmael lived in the desert, Hagar got a wife from Egypt for her son. In addition, Hagar and Ishmael learned to lower their expectations. As we all know, Abraham was rather well-off. It is probably fair to say that during the time Hagar and Ishmael had been living with Abraham, they would have lived quite comfortably. All of a sudden, they were cast out into the desert. They would have had to lower their expectations about the type of home they would live in, the food they could eat, the amount of attention that they could give to each other, and all of the other resources that they were used to. From the account of this story, it is apparent that the two lowered their expectation. (For instance Ishmael became an archer and provided food for himself and his mother.)

In our society many people are having to learn to lower the expec-

tations that they have of their loved ones. Mom has a friend who went back to work a few years ago. This woman, her husband, and their five children sat around the table to discuss how they could all help to fulfill this new plan. All of the children offered some of their time to complete tasks that the mother had done for so many years. For example, a couple of the teenagers said they would do the weekly grocery shopping. Another of the kids who had a driver's license said that she would pick up her younger sister every Tuesday. Finally, it came time for the husband to say what he would do for his wife. He said that he would lower his expectations of her in the home. This may sound trivial; however, when many wives start working outside of the home, they are still expected to complete everything inside the home that they did before they began their new jobs. However, when both parents are working the spouses and the children have to lower or change their expectations.

Also, Ishmael worked on his relationship with his brother. Though we don't know all the details, we remember that the two did not part on great terms. However, in Genesis 25:8-9 we read that both Isaac and Ishmael buried Abraham. In those days burial services included a lot of preparation, and the ceremony was quite long. Therefore, there must have been some sort of agreement made between these two so that together they could perform the tasks that were necessary to bury Abraham.

Now you may be saying that you have tried to fix specific relationships, but you just aren't getting anywhere. You are very committed to the other person and yet you don't get any response in return. First of all, you have to ask yourself if you are doing absolutely everything that you possibly can to make the relationship work. If not, then you can still work on it. However, if you are doing everything then take comfort in knowing that you are responsible for only your own actions. You aren't responsible for the way someone else reacts to you. All you have to do is make sure that you are doing everything possible to make sure that the relationship will work.

Commitment to a relationship may mean helping someone break the cycle. But how can you break the cycle of hurt and discouragement and begin again? Is it possible to break it? Some tell us it isn't. "Once you are born into a dysfunctional family, the cycle begins and can never be broken," they say. If that is true, all we can offer the victim is pity!

I happen to believe the Christian faith has a lot more to offer than pity. The cycle *can* be broken! God crashed the cycle in the person of Christ and made that possible. The Apostle Paul told us, "Therefore, if anyone is in Christ, he is a new creation; the old has gone, the new has come!" (2 Corinthians 5:17).

If all we have to work with is "old" people in the "old" cycle, then we are indeed in a whole heap of trouble! But if God can make the old people new people and help them to see "old" things in a new way, then He has created not only new creatures, but the possibility of those new creatures breaking out of determinism and beginning a brand-new cycle of their own!

I fully realize it may take time and expert help, counseling, and prayer, and in some cases, doctors and more extensive therapy; but when people are able to tap into the incredible resources of power and spiritual healing available because of Christ's death and resurrection, they are not only able to break the cycle of dysfunction for themselves, but eventually are able to help others to do it too. I like to think Hagar, who lived before a cross had ever been crafted to fit a man from Galilee, learned enough of all this to break her own particular cycle. If knowing so little, she achieved so much, then how do we who have so many advantages face her challenge? How can we help ourselves and our children to create a new cycle of freedom and love? We need to build values into our lives. Someone has said, "Values are a series of decisions based on what I think is important!" So Hagar obeyed God and went back home to submit herself to Sarai because God told her to do it. She believed God to be important and she valued what He said.

Values are something we all have. Each of us holds some things important. The source of some of our values, moreover, is tradition. Traditional behavior patterns are passed down from one generation to another. What my parents have deemed important can become important to me.

Some children were watching their parents preparing Thanksgiving dinner. The father cut off the ends of the ham and passed the meat to his wife. She took it from him, coated it with glaze, and placed it in a pan to bake.

"Why do you cut off both ends of the ham?" the youngsters asked their father.

"I really don't know," he replied "Grandma always did!"

The next Thanksgiving Day was at Grandma's house. The grandchildren came early, in time to see Grandma cut off both ends of the ham before she put it in the oven. They asked her the reason and Grandma replied, "I don't know; Nanna always cut the ends off like that." Now Nanna was still alive and kicking, and so the great-grandchildren had the chance to ask her their big question.

"Nanna, why do you cut off both ends of the Thanksgiving ham?"

"My baking pan is too small," the old lady replied simply!

How much influence we have on other people without even realizing it! If we assiduously "copy" our forebears in small matters that have assumed an importance through tradition (such as the way we cut up a ham), how much more do we copy their moral traditions? Such a story leads us to pause and ask ourselves, *Are the values of my environment, the traditions of my family important for me to keep? Or is it perhaps time to examine them and break the cycle?*

Christians will look at their values through Christ, filtering the things they count important through His Word, His standards. This way positive values picked up from others can be tried and tested, and new decisions can be made to drop harmful habits from our lives. Perhaps it would even help us to think of the word *priorities* instead of the word *values*.

Traditional priorities were extremely important in biblical days. This was the way tribes kept their distinctives. Stories were verbally passed through the generations, keeping memories alive. Advice and wise sayings and brave deeds would become part of a family's heritage. Stories would be told in the tent door about Joshua and Caleb who loved the Lord first, and children would be encouraged to model after Sarai who called her husband "Adonai"—Lord!

Take, for example, the wise words of the king of Massa, written in Proverbs 31. Few writings have so influenced the Christian woman who wants to find a model to follow. The passage contains advice on suitable kingly behavior; on what should matter *most* to a kingly king; and best known of all, the description of the noble woman "more precious than rubies." This woman of industry and compassion that Proverbs 31 describes for us is a busy businesswoman who adroitly juggles all her many activities while raising appreciative, godly children. But she is a woman who first and foremost fears the Lord and is praised for it!

Who do you think passed down all these wise sayings in this chapter of Scripture—this grand advice, this helpful instruction? The king of Massa wrote these words. He told us,

however, that these were sayings that his own mother had taught him, and presumably passed down by his mother's mother. Just where did Proverbs 31 have its birth? Well, the king of Massa was a direct descendent of Ishmael himself! I like to think that Hagar was able to get over her bitterness and hurt concerning her past and forgive her mistress Sarah and her master Abraham. I like to think the Lord helped her to pass along the traditions, truths, precepts, and priorities she had learned in Abraham's tent and through her harrowing, though shaping, experiences. The sorts of values we read about in Proverbs 31 are most certainly Judeo-Christian standards.

Hagar and Ishmael were apparently able to pick up their lives and get on with them. We have so little information concerning the details that followed once the Lord saved them in the desert, but we know the pair was able to draw on the strength of character and the values they had known. They were able to sort through them with the Lord's help and add new values and traditions of their very own as they built a new life together.

Human beings are amazingly resilient. Over and over again they were able to use all the building blocks that have been put into place in their lives to help them climb out of their holes. The temptation at such points in our personal history is to just lie down under our thornbush and expire with grief. Given a last chance Hagar and Ishmael took it and began to put their shattered lives back together again.

Think of a card game. When you are playing a card game, you accept whatever hand is dealt to you. You know there are a variety of "hands" around the table of life. You know too that some are better than others. So what do you do? Throw your hand at the dealer in a fit of rage or try to steal someone else's hand? No, you usually put every bit of ingenuity into winning with whatever hand you have been given.

Now winning—even with a "bad" hand—takes character. It takes love and support and, often times as we have already mentioned, expert advice and trained therapists, but it can be done. Hagar and Ishmael did it! They didn't throw in their hands and refuse to play. They did the best they could with a bad "deal" and God did the rest!

COMMITMENT

TALK TIME

1. Read Proverbs 31.
   What part of this advice had the most impact on you?
   Discuss why that piece of advice struck you so strongly.

2. Discuss the following quotation.
   "Once you are born into a dysfunctional family, the cycle begins and can never be broken," they say. If that is true, all we can offer the victim is pity! I happen to believe the Christian faith has a lot more to offer than pity. The cycle can be broken! God crashed the cycle in the person of Christ and made that possible. The Apostle Paul told us, 'Therefore, if anyone is in Christ, he is a new creation; the old is gone, the new has come!' (2 Corinthians 5:17)."

THINK TIME

1. Look over the chapter headings and decide which one best relates to you.
   Confusion
   Conflicts
   Coping
   Community
   Change
   Communion
   Caring
   Commitment

2. Proverbs 31:30 says, "A woman who fears the Lord is to be praised."
   What do you think "the fear of the Lord" means?
   How do you think the fear of the Lord can strengthen relationships?

3. Write a personal note to the Lord about the hand you have been dealt in life. Give Him the note in prayer.

PRAYER TIME

1. Pray for those who have given up hope that the dysfunctional cycle they are in will ever be broken. Pray that they may find hope in the Christ who can make the difference!

2. Pray for the resource people in your town who are trying to minister to others.

3. Pray for more godly resources to be made available.

4. Pray for yourself and your family.

ACTION TIME

1. Christ is your ultimate resource. Learn to fly first to Him when trouble comes, and ask Him to lead you to the "human" resource most helpful to you.

2. Church resources:

   Fellowship. Be in a small group where you are known, supported, prayed for, and can be yourself.

   Worship. Make sure you are regularly praising God in the company of His people.

   Bible study.
   Try to develop your own personal quiet time with God.
   Be in a small group of people learning how to discover for themselves the truths of God from the Scriptures.

   Prayer partners. Try to find a prayer partner. This can be an incredible source of strength for you.

Books and tapes. Visit a Christian bookstore. Ask for recommendations of good books on the particular need you have.

3. Community resources (see your local yellow pages)